"This book will challenge ... date that is imperative for the ... eady convinced—that discipleship is not a program we launch, but a lifestyle we embrace. Jonathan's words will equip you, beloved saint, for the work of the ministry. We are grateful for Jonathan's insights and writing, which have helped to accelerate our mission at Manhood Journey. I'm delighted to recommend his book to any believer who wants to faithfully serve our great King!"

—Kent Evans,
Executive Director, Manhood Journey,
Author of *Wise Guys: Unlocking Hidden Wisdom from the Men Around You*

"Spiritual growth is not an option—it's a biblical mandate. Jonathan makes this case in *Ordinary Radicals*, calling Christians to reach greater heights with Jesus. If you're wondering whether your church is on the right path in discipling its congregation, start here. If you want to personally start discipling others, this book will affirm your desire and help you take the first step."

—Tom Harper,
CEO, Networld Media Group,
Author of *Through Colored Glasses: How Great Leaders Reveal Reality*

"*Ordinary Radicals* is a simple, straightforward guide for ordinary people that will equip them to live as faithful disciples of Jesus Christ. A great choice for a new members' class in your church!"

—Timothy Paul Jones, PhD,
Professor of Christian Family Ministry,
The Southern Baptist Theological Seminary

"In an era where there is much confusion or even apathy about discipleship, Jonathan Hayashi gives us a simple and yet powerful explanation of discipleship centered around the person of Jesus. If you are serious about Jesus and being shaped into his image, you should pay attention to this book."

—Micah Fries,
Senior Pastor of Brainerd Baptist Church, Chattanooga, Tennessee,
Author and Editor, *Islam and North America*

"If you are looking for a quick and easy program to turn around your church, stop looking; there is no such thing. With biblical clarity and Holy Spirit-fueled passion, Jonathan Hayashi has written a clarion call to church leaders to remind us of our purpose: fulfilling the Great Commission and the Great Commandment. So much of Western church culture claims the name of Christ, yet refuses to follow His pattern of making disciples. Jonathan reminds us that Christians follow Christ and that Christ made disciples who made disciples. I'm a firm believer that belief determines behavior, so if you believe in Jesus, you must obey his command. This book will help you align belief and behavior."

—**Dr. Adron Robinson,**
Pastor of Hillcrest Baptist Church,
President of Illinois Baptist State Association (IBSA)

"Jonathan Hayashi will make you think differently about discipleship. His book *Ordinary Radicals* challenges popular assumptions about what it means to follow Jesus. His basic assertion is that discipleship is not optional. To be a Christian is to be a disciple. If following Christ is important to you, this book will give you a vision of what it means to be an ordinary radical for Jesus."

—**Dr. John Koessler,**
Professor of Applied Theology & Church Ministry, Moody Bible Institute,
Author of *True Discipleship: The Art of Following Jesus*

"Trained by some of the most respected disciple-makers, Jonathan Hayashi offers to his readers an articulate distillation of the principles necessary for making disciples while being faithful to the gospel. *Ordinary Radicals: A Return to Christ-Centered Discipleship* has the potential to be a valuable resource for local churches and many groups in the Christian community."

—**Dr. John Yeats,**
Executive Director, Missouri Baptist Convention,
Recording Secretary, Southern Baptist Convention

"Over the years, I have watched Jonathan Hayashi consistently serve his local church with the same passion that is now evident in this new call for "ordinary radicals." Comfortable Christians will be stirred by this challenge and then encouraged by the clear path forward that Jonathan outlines, as it leads to a deeper level of discipleship and the inevitable result of a greater Gospel advance. May the radical discipleship to which he is calling us become more and more ordinary, for the glory of God and the advance of His mission and kingdom."

—**Nate Adams,**
Executive Director, Illinois Baptist State Association

"Jonathan hits the nail on the head when he shares that too many churches today have a program-driven mentality. They have more books, podcasts, and resources available than ever before, yet they are failing to create witnessing, multiplying churches. You'll be motivated and encouraged by *Ordinary Radicals* to get back to discipleship through equipping others to discover the joy of joining God in fulfilling the Great Commission by making genuine disciples of Jesus Christ."

—**Rev. John B. Sorensen, DD, DHL,**
President/CEO, Evangelism Explosion International

ORDINARY RADICALS

A RETURN TO CHRIST-CENTERED DISCIPLESHIP

JONATHAN HAYASHI

LUCIDBOOKS

I dedicate this book to Jason Walter, a faithful follower of Christ, my friend and mentor, and a faithful servant who displays the likeness of Christ in every way. He inspires me to be a better follower of Christ, a husband who gives sacrificially, and a father to my beautiful children. To the one who fearlessly proclaims Christ and encouraged me to believe I was capable of writing this book.

Table of Contents

Special Thanks

This book was completed in large part due to the urgency I have sensed in the task of disciple-making, which was made known in my circle of fellow clergy in the state of Missouri. I am humbled and thankful to my Lord Jesus Christ who saved me from the depth of my sin and purchased me with His own blood. I am grateful that God has given me the opportunity to be a disciple-maker so I can train others by using this book for the furtherance of His gospel.

I thank God for Leslie Korhammer for her detailed editing work in the early manuscript, Nathan Street for a thorough theological edit, Rebekah Schwartz for her marketing side as a videographer, Jessica Claborn for her time in setting the author page online, Skyler Julian for his service in using social media to spread the word, and finally, Laura Tiffany for her ecstatic work in graphic design with the front cover of this book.

I thank the Lord for placing me in a family with a godly mother, Yukiko Hayashi, who faithfully modeled Christ-likeness in the home. At age 16, I came to know the saving grace of Jesus Christ because of her diligence and patience in the gospel witness with prayer and fasting. My growth in love for the church and for Christ's word was evident in the early years of my spiritual journey. I praise God for the major milestone in my family when my father, Takakazu Hayashi, came to know the saving grace of Jesus Christ in 2012.

I am forever grateful for my loving, affirming siblings who have spoken truth in love into my life. I thank God for Takayuki Hayashi, who serves as a pastor missionary; Kazuyuki Hayashi for his diligence in careful articulate study as a seminary professor and PhD student; and Chrissy Hayashi for the impact she has had on my family and her faithful mission work in Japan. I would not be where I am today in full-time ministry in the local church if it were not for the encouragement and prayer I received from my siblings.

Finally, to say that I am grateful for my wonderful wife is a gross understatement. She continues to show me grace, patience, kindness, and love. Words are not enough to begin to describe how grateful I am for her, the mother of our children, my dearest friend, and my closest companion. Kennedi has supported me with her steadfast love and causes me daily to want to walk and grow more in Christ-likeness. I am also thankful for our two beautiful daughters, Kaede Selah and Annah Karis, as we continue grow as a family.

My hope and prayer are that this book will serve and equip the saints in the local church to begin a world revolution through the local movement of the gospel for the sake of the gospel.

Jonathan Hayashi
Troy, Missouri

Foreword

We parent the way that we've been parented, we teach the way that we've been taught, we lead the way that we've been led, and most importantly, we disciple the way that we've been discipled—if we were even discipled in the first place.

Imagine if on this Sunday—assuming that you're not preaching—the Kids Director grabs you and asks if you could sub in for a sick teacher. "I haven't taught children for years," you respond, "in fact, I don't even know how good of a parent I am in the first place!"

She replies, "You're fine, it's really not that hard. We have the lesson here, so all you have to do is keep their attention and teach it."

"Teaching it is not the problem . . ." you mutter under your breath as you reluctantly walk into a class full of six-year-olds.

How would you teach them? What would you do? What if they don't pay attention? How would you get their attention?

Would you flicker the lights on and off, like one of your Sunday school teachers might've done? Would you clap a rhythmic cheer to capture their attention and get them to be silent, like your schoolteacher might've done? Or, would you raise one hand and put the other to your mouth, to signal that they're too loud like the Kids Director usually does?

Unless you consciously do otherwise, you will likely teach those children the way that you were taught when you were a child. It's not because you studied textbooks on adolescent development or conducted longitudinal research on children that you would act this way—it's just because this is what "normal" is to you.

Unfortunately (or fortunately), we do the same thing when it comes to discipleship. This is because we disciple the way that we've been discipled. If you were discipled by a disciple-maker, then great! You likely understand 2 Timothy 2:2 and the importance of spiritual multiplication. If not, then you might think that cultivating your relationship with Christ is all that you're required to do.

In both cases, *Ordinary Radicals* is going to help move you from wherever you are, to where God is calling you to be. In other words, in this book, Jonathan acts as a tour guide, rather than a travel agent. Instead of pointing you to where you need to be, he's going to guide you and your church in the direction toward Christ. After all, it's like I say in my book, *No Silver Bullets*, "Disciples are not made when they get to a destination. Disciples are formed *while moving* toward Christ."[1] This is because discipleship is about direction, not destination.

This isn't a book to be read by the fireplace or on a beach by yourself. It's a book that you need to read, take notes on, and use as you work with your team. So, buckle up, and let's learn how to become ordinary radicals.

Daniel Im

Introduction

Every church needs to answer two questions.
First, what is our plan for making disciples?
And second, does our plan work?

—Dallas Willard

A few summers ago, I woke up one morning and sensed the Lord pressing my heart with a great burden. I got up and did the usual—poured my coffee, grabbed my bag, hopped into my vehicle, and drove to the office. It was early, and I was the only one in the office, so I opened my Bible and read as I normally did each day. Although God's word often brings me peace, this day my mind was spinning and stirring.

As I looked out the window of my office, I couldn't help but think that somewhere along the way we had missed the mark. There was a real sense of uneasiness in my heart, and I wanted to simply drop everything and move on to something else. Going through the motions, checking off church responsibilities and opportunities like a checklist, going to Sunday school—I knew there had to be more than that. Is being a Christian simply being involved with a bunch of church activities? It made no sense to me.

1

There had to be more to the Christian life than "God loves you and offers a wonderful plan for your life"[1] and then moving on. Handing out tracts at the mall just didn't seem like the fullness of Christian discipleship. That's real good stuff, but man, there seemed to be a gap that didn't make sense. I mean, people are dying and going to hell without ever hearing the gospel of their own salvation. We clearly have no time to waste our lives. I am thinking about the area and the city I live in where thousands of people surround me. How can I make my life count for them and for Christ? I don't want to waste this life that has been entrusted to me. I want this life to count for His glory.

> I knew there had to be more than that. Is being a Christian simply being involved with a bunch of church activities?

We've Missed the Point

Here's the reality. Churches have too often failed because of three lies—ignorance, uncertainty, and lack of self-value. When Christians believe these lies, it hinders and keeps believers from pursuing the discipleship call of Christ. Throughout history, God has done extraordinary things through ordinary people—ordinary radicals.

You may be thinking this: What on earth is an ordinary radical? That's an oxymoron. I will explain further in the chapters that will unfold, so hang in there with me. But as you have noticed already, in many of our churches, the ordinary Christian will always fight the status quo of lukewarm Christianity. Throughout the scriptures, God calls His people in the midst of a crooked generation to be the people of faith and step out (Phil. 2:15). This is a radical stand that goes against our fleshly desire (Gal. 5:17). However, it is such a shame and grieves my heart that it has become a norm to live a nominal, casual Christianity.

At times, I wonder why the church has so little influence on the world. What has happened to the church? God then convicted my heart and showed me that it is because the world has so much influence on the church. Study after study reveals that professing Christians look no different than the world.[2] We find that abortion in the church is just as prevalent as outside in the world. We find that divorce is just as prevalent. We find immorality everywhere. We look pretty much identical to non-Christians in the way we spend our lives and use our time. We pour our souls into the things the world tells us are good and the most important on this Earth; namely, speaking, sports, and entertainment. We spend hours practicing for this and that, hours on video games, hours in front of a TV, and minutes, at the most, in God's word or in prayer. The effects are evident.

> At times I wonder why the church has so little influence on the world. What has happened to the church? God then convicted my heart and showed me that it is because the world has so much influence on the church.

John Piper once tweeted, "One of the great uses of Twitter and Facebook will be to prove at the Last Day that prayerlessness was not from lack of time."[3] We use social media, text, and talk on mere temporal conversations with people who are going to spend eternity in either heaven or hell.

I am convinced that the greatest need of the church today is more men, women, boys, and girls who will abandon their dreams, possessions, and treasures at the feet of the cross and rise up to be the disciples that the scripture points us to and multiply the gospel to the ends of the Earth (Acts 1:8).

To be a disciple of Jesus is to make disciples of Jesus (Mark 16:15). Discipleship is not a call for others to come to us to hear the gospel, but a command for us to go to others to share the gospel (Rom. 10:14–15). Jesus has not given us an option to consider but a command to obey. If we won't go, who will?

> Jesus has not given us an option to consider but a command to obey. If we won't go, who will?

Unfolding this Book

This book begins with this fundamental question: Where are we? Chapter 1 beckons the question of the dilemma many churches are facing. Chapter 2 then begins with the foundation of the gospel. Every chapter explains another essential aspect in the process of discipleship. Please don't think this book is a to-do list and move on to the other tasks in order to grow your church. At the core of this book is the gospel that drives every strategy, structure, and system. Apart from the gospel, all skill sets and styles of best-shared valued leadership are based on sinking sand and will eventually crumble. The task of discipleship is grounded and founded in Christ, which the title gives away—a return to Christ-centered discipleship.

The book will then ask this question: Where are we headed? Chapter 3 shows the path of Jesus as an intentional leader; Chapter 4 looks into the vehicle of the local church through the relational environment; and Chapter 5 deals with the roadmap of biblical blueprint. Once again, with the foundation of the gospel built from the bottom up, we are then able to step midstream into the pragmatics of the mission. Without a proper vision, the task of discipleship will perish (Prov. 29:18). As an old Japanese proverb says, "A vision without an action is a daydream. An action without vision is a nightmare."[4] No strategy (mission) of making disciples can bring profound, lasting change unless the vision is rooted in the gospel.

This book closes with the final question: Where will we end up? Chapter 6 speaks of the call for all disciples to carry out the Great Commission. Chapter 7 teaches the radical measure of obedience in discipleship. Chapter 8 speaks of the multiplication movement that brings exponential growth. I want to encourage readers not to jump directly into Chapter 8, since the root foundation is the gospel, which will be evident throughout this entire book. Taking the slow steps will bring lasting, long-term change as you consider the gospel in your life.

This book is for anyone who is wrestling with nominal, casual Christianity (Matt. 15:7–9). Even though I've probably never met many of you who are reading this book, I feel like I know you. I've been there and walked through the same journey toward change for the sake of the gospel. If our church ends up looking like every other struggling church, what are we really accomplishing? I feel and sense the desire to see the change for the sake of guilty, needy, perishing sinners around you. This book is about taking the Great Commission mandate in every aspect of our lives, being consumed and ablaze in adoration, causing us to reach out in love to the lost, perishing world (Matt. 9:37–38). By the end of the book, you will not only be able to explain why making disciples is a priority for both you and your church, but will also be equipped and ready to go make disciples of all nations.

This book will unfold with these honest, open-hearted questions: How do we think and take root the gospel in our very lives? Why bother with discipleship? The cost of non-discipleship is too great. To live with radical abandonment for His glory, faithful adherence to His person, urgent obedience to His ministry—that is costly. With this book, I would like to offer a step-by-step process for readers to jump into the task of the Great Commission in order to begin the world revolution through a local movement of the gospel.

My Prayer for All Who Read This Book

I pray that the army of believers who read this book will radically and without hesitation begin this movement of discipleship reformation. I pray this movement will sweep this land of ordinary people and cause them to live a life of discipleship.

I pray that God will sweep our churches with a wind of great awakening for the call to discipleship in this dark, sin-stained world in desperate need of the gospel. The time has come for a new kind of discipleship, a radical discipleship by ordinary radicals. My prayer is that people will see that following Jesus costs everything you are and everything you have. And my prayer is that people will see that Jesus is worth it and that He is more than enough.

Where Are We?

Chapter 1

Evangelism Discipleship Dilemma

Why is evangelism not enough to fulfill the Great Commission?

—Jonathan Hayashi

News flash: American churches are in crisis.[1] According to the Southern Baptist Convention (SBC), recent stats shared at the annual SBC conference 2017 in Phoenix, Arizona, revealed a decline in membership, baptisms, average worship attendance, and total giving. Nearly 4,000 churches close every year in North America.

Several years ago, in *Transformational Church*, a book published by Lifeway Christian Researchers Thom Rainer and Ed Stetzer, a study of 2,300 churches sponsored by 15 denominations revealed staggering numbers. Fewer than half of those churches said they had any plan in place for discipling people, and only 60 percent had someone responsible for any level of spiritual formation among children, students, and adults.[2] Stetzer estimates that 70 percent to 80 percent of all evangelical churches in the United States have either stopped growing or are in decline.[3]

I am grieved that churches are clearly losing the effectiveness of discipleship. It's no mystery at all to say that the world we live in is in trouble. That's an understatement. What has gone wrong with the harvest? What is happening with our evangelical circles to cause the decline of conversion and discipleship?

Few Attempt to Fix the Problem: Information Leads to Transformation

I know what we need. Let's come up with better curriculum and better sermons. What is interesting is that churches have more books and podcasts available than ever before, but they're failing at witnessing. In the Millennial generation with high technological advancement, people have more access to information than ever before. Churches have more conferences than ever, more sermons at their fingertips, more books than you can read in a lifetime, yet they have fewer conversions, baptisms, and commitments to make disciples. Indeed, we have more than enough resources, but we are failing to fulfill the Great Commission.

Too many churches have a program-driven mentality. They seem to think that if we listen to more sermons and read enough books, then somehow people will be changed.

That's the human paradigm—we better ourselves hoping that as we become better, others magically will, too. But Jesus directs us to teach others.

Now please don't get me wrong. Events and programs aren't bad. But when people depend on them to do all the work of discipling rather than focusing on individuals, we should expect them to eventually fail. When believers look to the life of Christ, they see that He not only taught but also led the disciples in real-life training on the field (Matt. 17:14–20). Knowledge in itself puffs up and is not good (1 Cor. 8:1). Most Christian leaders have a head full of information about the Bible. Knowledge without application results in less than radical disciples (James 2:14–26). The more we know, the less time we have to apply what we are learning (1 John 2:17). It's not what we know that will change the world; it's how we love others and share the gospel (good news) that will ultimately win back the effectiveness of missional outreach (Gal. 6:7). In his book *Deliberate Simplicity: How the Church Does More by Doing Less*, Dave Browning said that "the gap holding back most believers is not the gap between what they know and what they don't know. It's the gap between what they know and what they're living."[4] We have become educated beyond our obedience.

My time in seminary was perhaps one of the most formative times in my spiritual journey. Higher education has prepared many like me for full-time ministry. But seminary didn't teach me everything. I didn't know how to make disciples. I mean, on a theoretical level yes, but nothing on the practical level. I learned how to grasp good theology, but that led to bad methodology. I was absolutely lost as I dealt in my own personal attempt to live as a disciple-maker to make disciples who made disciples. Today, seminary students are taught how to preach but not know how to make disciples. There are evangelism classes but not the practical application for how to make disciples who make disciples.

As a seminary student studying to become a pastor, I was memorizing Matthew 28:19–20 for a class requirement: "Go therefore and make disciples of all nations, baptizing them in the name of the Father," and then it dawned on me. Jonathan, you may have been a Christian as long as you can remember, and you have gone to seminary for

> You may have been a Christian as long as you can remember, and you have gone to seminary for three years, but have you baptized somebody? Have you ever made even one disciple?

three years, but have you baptized somebody? Have you ever made even one disciple? I thought for a moment, and then I made excuses. *Well, it's not time to do that right now. It's study time to get ready for the future, and it's a time to get away.*

However, deep down, I knew my excuses didn't make any sense. Knowing that people I walked by in my city, just a block away from my church, might spend an eternity separated from God didn't seem right. Shouldn't I do something about it? There seemed to be a gap between these simple Christian thoughts and the eternal reality at risk. It made no sense to me. People are dying and going to hell without ever hearing the gospel.

The Disputed Dilemma of the Call for Churches

I was recently in a conversation that went like this: "Well, I know discipleship is important, but I'm really just for the lost." I don't think this person understood what it meant for followers of Christ to carry out the Great Commission. I mean, is discipleship a choice for the Christian, or a necessary part of being a Christian? As Christians, it seems as though we use those terms, *Christian* and *disciple*, as if they mean different things.

The person I was talking to continued and asked something like this: "So wait, aren't we supposed to just reach people? Then why focus inward on our own little business by discipling? Which one is more important? Evangelism or discipleship?"

Surely, both are important. The tension is real, and as a result, people generally often go the safe route by just saying that both are important. However, if someone were to insist on an answer and persist, I would have to choose discipleship. The reason is that when we look at the Great Commission (Matt. 28:18–20), Jesus told His followers to make disciples, not converts.

I am not against conversion and evangelism. But conversion is just the first step in being a disciple. If the church exists simply for that reason, baptism becomes the finish line rather than the starting line. Disciple-making is the end means of it all.

But I guess the question is this: Why do we separate discipleship and evangelism? Let me ask you an interesting question I heard while I was in seminary: When did the disciples become Christians? The answer can differ, but I believe it was at Pentecost (Acts 2:1–18). So let's backtrack a bit. Not to have an over-reductionist observation, but it seems that according to Christ's model, discipleship came first (Matt. 4:19) with the selection of the 12 disciples. Evangelism came after (Matthew 28:19) with the commissioning of the 12 disciples.

Did Jesus select his disciples even before they were believers? This is a counter cultural model.[5] We tend to think evangelism first, then discipleship. In the early church, we see the gospel shared, disciples made, churches planted, and elders appointed (Acts 14:1–28). We see the opposite plan today. Looking at the biblical model, we see how far we've moved.[6]

Bursting the Myth of Discipleship

Discipleship has turned into a buzzword that too many are throwing around without properly defining it. The crisis is that it seems like we have a whole Tower of Babel effect of what discipleship is all about. It seems as though we say the word *discipleship*, but we are speaking different languages to one another.

Dietrich Bonhoeffer was a professor, pastor, theologian, and spy during the reign of Hitler's Nazi Germany in the 1930s and 1940s. He died a martyr, but before he died, he said, "Christianity without discipleship is always Christianity without Christ."[7] He believed that unless one followed Christ in a serious fashion, it cheapened the grace of God.

Why? Because our assumption is wrong, which leads to a shaky foundation that ultimately makes the entire structure falter. Therefore, I'm coming back to the

> Why? Because our assumption is wrong, which leads to a shaky foundation that ultimately makes the entire structure falter.

bedrock, foundational root of what is a disciple of Christ and what it means to make disciples.

What Is Discipleship?

Today, with much innovation and new strategies entering church leadership, sometimes it's hard to navigate and define the basic principle of discipleship. The English word *discipleship* actually never occurs in the Bible; however, defining a disciple is fairly easy. The Greek word μανθάνω is the word scripture uses for *disciple*, and it means "to learn."

Discipleship is the entire process of salvation, from conversion to baptism to instruction in the ways of Jesus (Matt. 28:19–20). In other words, disciples are people who learn to be like Jesus and do what Jesus could do. As we see in the New Testament book of Acts, "When they had preached the gospel to that city and had made many disciples, they returned to Lystra and to Iconium and to Antioch" (Acts 14:21). Scripture teaches that an alive Christian is a growing Christian (2 Pet. 1:8–10). Scripture also teaches that we grow not only by instruction but by imitation (1 Cor. 4:16, 11:1).

Therefore, discipleship is a process of disciples called to know Christ, grow with Christ, and go for Christ.[8] This is a never-ending process; you will never be finished as a disciple of Christ. We like to think this way: I make disciples every week. After all, 600 people hear my preaching every Sunday. However, Jesus counters the human model in Matthew 4:19. He didn't say, "Therefore, I invite you to grab a pen and a pew as we go through an eight-week sermon series on discipleship."[9] Many pastors think their greatest impact comes from preaching to many. Not true. Our greatest impact is in discipling a few. Jesus did life with the disciples in close proximity. You won't create radical disciples from a pulpit; you'll only create an audience. You must walk closely with people. Daniel Im said it another way. A disciple-maker must move from being a sage on the stage to a guide on the side.[10]

We cannot change the definition of discipleship to mean sitting and listening and then expect people to make disciples. In Jesus's model, you will always have room to grow and mature. This biblical definition of discipleship

> Many pastors think their greatest impact comes from preaching to many. Not true. Our greatest impact is in discipling a few.

should be a natural and vital part of the local congregation that looks to Christ. Jesus's method has simply been ignored.

This is a radical, countercultural view for many of our churches. Discipleship occurs when someone answers the call to learn from Jesus how to live his or her life as though Jesus were living it. Radical Christians are those who hear the word of God and faithfully walk in the footsteps of Christ, making disciples by going, baptizing, and teaching people the scripture and passing this lesson on to the next generation.

Do *Christian* and *Disciple* Mean Different Things?

I recently visited a few men at the church I pastor, and at the close of our conversation, I asked, "What does it mean to be a disciple of Jesus?" A couple of the men paused and thought about it, but one responded, "Disciples are not followers of Jesus." I was puzzled by this answer. He continued, "Well, Muslims are followers of Jesus because they think he was a good prophet. Judas Iscariot followed Jesus, but He wasn't a follower of Jesus. When Jesus called His disciples and said, 'Follow me,' that was pre-ascension of Christ, pre-Pentecost, pre-birth of the church, and pre-sealing of the Holy Spirit." Wait, so is discipleship a choice for the Christian, or a necessary part of being a Christian?

Shockingly, as I interviewed many more people in our church, I soon noticed there were many different definitions of a disciple.

It seemed that no one knew what a simple definition of a disciple was. Christians tend to use the terms *Christian* and *disciple* as if they mean different things. We must first know what a disciple is in order to make one in the process of discipleship.

Interestingly, the best way to answer that question is to focus not on the concept of a disciple but on the identity of Jesus. In order to understand what it means to live as followers of Jesus, we must first have a proper view of Jesus.

Discipleship is first deeply rooted in the doctrine of union with Christ. Our salvation was not ours to begin with; redemption has been accomplished by Christ, through Christ, and in Christ. Therefore, discipleship is the work of disciples accomplished by the Holy Spirit by grace through faith. Christ works through us, pointing ultimately to Himself in the inner working of the Holy Spirit. Consider these verses:

- Romans 5:17 – "For if, because of one man's trespass, death reigned through that one man, much more will those who receive the abundance of grace and the free gift of righteousness reign in life through the one man Jesus Christ."
- 2 Corinthians 5:17 – "Therefore, if anyone is in Christ, he is a new creation. The old has passed away; behold, the new has come."
- Galatians 2:20 – "I have been crucified with Christ. It is no longer I who live, but Christ who lives in me."

The definition of a disciple is found in Matthew 4:18–22. Being a disciple always leads to making a disciple. From the very beginning of Christianity when Jesus said, "Follow me, and I will make you to become fishers of men" (Matt. 4:19), there have been three characteristics of a disciple: cognition, affection, and volition. Therefore, a disciple is one who, with their head, follows the call to the person of Christ, one whose heart is transformed into the likeness of Christ, and whose hands begin to multiply for the glory of Christ.

The whole picture is that Jesus is saying what it means to be a disciple. It's so much more than following certain rules, paths, or regulations. It is Jesus saying follow into a personal relationship with me and become more and more like me. That is what it means to be my disciple. Karl Barth said it well: "Follow me is the substance of the call in the power of which Jesus makes people his saints…. We may say, therefore, that in practice the command to follow Jesus is identified with the command to believe in him."[11] Therefore, within that command itself, it is the work of God causing us to follow Him. Therefore, faith in itself is not man's gift unto man, but God's gift unto man.

It is the idea of rebirth in His followers. As we see in this New Testament narrative account, contextually, Jesus is walking by the shore of the Sea of Galilee. He sees Peter and Andrew in the boat and calls them to abandon their dreams, plans, priorities, treasures, possessions, and pleasures of this world and follow Him. In response, Peter and Andrew, with absolute submission, immediately left their nets and followed him (Matt. 4:20). In many cases, we see quite the opposite. When Jesus called for a similar surrender, the majority of the crowd deserted and left Jesus (Mark 14:50). Those who followed this radical call are known as the 12 disciples (Matt. 10:2–3).[12] There was no such thing as halfway carnal disciples, according to Jesus. In fact, John the disciple said Jesus will spit them out (Rev. 3:14–22). As Matthew's Gospel unfolds, we see that Jesus did not ignore the crowds; He was primarily engaged in teaching the 12 disciples. Even when He ministered to the thousands, it was in the context of teaching those disciples.

Peter, Andrew, James, and John were fishermen, all involved in family businesses, living in Capernaum or nearby Bethsaida (John 1:44). That was apparently also the home of Matthew at the time of his calling and of Philip and possibly Nathanael (John 1:43–45). The fishing profession in that day probably carried with it the same kind of social stigma that common labor does today. Three of the four (Peter, James, and John) would become Jesus's closest earthly friends. Andrew played a significant role in Christ's ministry more than once (Mark 13:3; John 1:40, 6:8, 12:22).

A disciple, according to Paul, is one who is an apprentice to Jesus (Phil. 3:7–11). Discipleship is all about learning from Jesus how to live our lives as though He were living in us. It is becoming the kind of person who naturally wills what Jesus wills. This is the mission Jesus entrusted to his followers and to us. Jesus prayed for this moment as he sweat blood before his death in the Garden of Gethsemane (John 17:26). C. S. Lewis said in his most famous work, *Mere Christianity*, "The Church exists for nothing else but to draw men into Christ, to make them little Christs. If they are not doing that, all the cathedrals, clergy, missions, sermons, even the Bible itself, are simply a waste of time. God became Man for no other purpose."[13] In essence, by definition, a disciple is a Christian. So, if you would, discipleship is Christianship or Christformity.[14]

The Local Church with the Great Commission

Discipleship is not the new cutting-edge, trendy, hip, cool thing churches are doing. The strategy is not new. This is not a new concept; it's as old as the Old Testament.[15] I believe with all my heart that a return to biblical discipleship will ignite the twenty-first century reformation.

When the local church becomes nothing about the Great Commission, it ceases to be what Christ has intended it to be. As Thom Rainer said, "Thriving churches have the Great Commission as the centerpiece of their vision, while dying churches have forgotten the clear command of Christ."[16] Discipleship has been cast aside. So when the church becomes an end in itself, it all ends.

Every church should embrace the mission of making disciples and implement a strategy to accomplish that mission. Because the mission of a local church is to make disciples, a strategy is how the church is designed to make disciples. If a church's strategy is not grounded in making disciples, the church has abandoned the mission Christ has given it.

The Urgency of the Gospel and Disciple-Making

There hasn't been a more crucial time than now for the church to rise up. We live in a fast-paced world, but we have only 52 Sundays a year. Discipleship requires urgency.

At the end of the day, it is a matter of obedience. People don't want to give in to the audacity of radical discipleship. If your church doesn't, then you have found the problem. Take your Bible and go off and don't return until your heart burns to become more like Jesus. This is the "cheap grace" that Dietrich Bonhoeffer called "the deadly enemy of our Church."[17]

> Why make disciples? Because heaven and hell exist, and the end of the world is coming.

Why make disciples? Because heaven and hell exist, and the end of the world is coming. We don't have time to play the same old game in our churches. The reality is that people need to be converted and taught about Christ. Think, feel, and act like a disciple, as a follower of Jesus. Embrace Him as Lord and savior.

Chapter 2

Gospel Hermeneutics

The health of the church is Hermeneutic of the gospel.

—Lesslie Newbigin

Recently, secular journalist Diana West wrote a book called *The Death of the Grown-Up*, where she cataloged the shift in Western culture over the last 10 years. The book has some fascinating statistics:

- Nearly one of three 30-year-olds has not left their parents' home.
- According to a survey, there are more adults today in America ages 18–49 who watch Cartoon Network more than they watch CNN.
- The average video gamester in 1990 was 18; today, it's 35, spending 20 hours per week playing video games.
- The National Academy of Sciences has redefined adolescence (the onset of puberty and adulthood) as lasting from ages 12 to 30 years old.
- The McArthur Foundation funded a research study conducted several years ago that argues that early adulthood does not end until age 34 in the Western world.[1]

As I pastor and grow older, I am more convinced that we need more men and women who are willing to grow old—not just to age, but to grow old well and model adulthood to younger generations. This idea of growing old is not only good, but it is essential in the church and in our ministry. Moving from immaturity to maturity (1 Pet. 2:2), going from milk to meat (1 Cor. 3:2, Heb. 5:12), is the biblical analogy of growing old (1 Cor. 14:20), aging well (Gal. 4:1–3).

Older Christian doesn't automatically mean mature Christian. In fact, those with whom you most likely have conflicts within your church are probably older people who never grew up. Old age doesn't necessarily make a person more faithful or more civil.

If we're honest, our behavior doesn't always match our belief system. How is that possible? It is easy to say we believe something simply because we think of it from time to time. We live in a false dichotomy. We think that how a person responds to an idea or situation in thought is how they would respond in behavior (lifestyle).

You know something is a bit off, although no one seems to know why. The question being raised is perhaps this: Why are so many people not growing deeper in their relationship with God?

This is a gospel issue. Here is the question we must ask: Do we truly and fully have a crystal-clear definition and understanding of the gospel? If so, do we live in such a way that demonstrates the gospel, and do people see how we live and that we love Jesus with all our beings?

Where the Problem Lies

Today, the American church is living in a bubble of false delusion about the meaning of the gospel and discipleship. The problem is that we don't really understand or know the gospel. If we are not preaching the biblical gospel, we are preaching what Paul would call a different gospel. A complete understanding of the gospel means we cannot divorce discipleship from the gospel (2 Cor. 11:4). I believe many Christians today believe a perverse gospel (Gal. 1:7–8).

Therefore, we have been caught in a hurricane of a lie, believing a false gospel (Eph. 4:14).

In the eighteenth century, Charles H. Spurgeon was noted as the supreme example of a true preacher. The scope of his ministry spread broader than any other man of his day.[2] Spurgeon would have been repulsed by manipulation or human-centered emotional methods in evangelism, which we call today *eisegesis* (Col. 3:23). Yet no one would have ever accused him of proclaiming the gospel without persuasion or passion (Rom. 15:20). The gospel, rightly proclaimed, is persuasive (Acts 2:14–41). And such a gospel, when believed due to the regenerating work of the Holy Spirit (Rom. 3:11, 1 Cor. 2:14), produces true disciples (John 3:5). uganda story

Being a Christian today sadly has no connection with being formed into the image of Christ (Rom. 8:29). The apostle Paul constantly reflected on his example and his walk. He said that what others saw in him, they were to pass on to others (Phil. 4:9). He constantly writes on the subject of imitation (1 Cor. 4:16). As Scott McKnight wrote in his book *The King Jesus Gospel*, "What I heard was that you can have the one without the other—that you can be saved and not be a disciple. I smelled a theological rat in that claim."[3]

The gospel you believe determines what kind of disciple you become. For example, if you believe in a legalistic gospel (do this, don't do that—the words that characterized the Pharisees), you become a legalistic disciple. If you believe in a liberal gospel (just love, love, love—we don't have any theology, and it doesn't matter because love wins—scripture is optional), you become a liberal disciple. If you believe in a prosperity gospel (God's love is determined by your wealth, health, and prosperity, and you have a sense of entitlement to boost your selfish ego), you become a prosperity disciple. Therefore, the gospel has everything to do with discipleship. It's not either-or—it is both. Several of these ideas are taken from Bill Hull in his book *Conversion & Discipleship*.[4]

1. Forgiveness-Only Gospel

The most common gospel preached today focuses almost exclusively on the forgiveness-only gospel. Why is it so popular? Because it's so easy and simple. For many churches, the understanding of the gospel too often is a transactional model.

The term *Christian* tends to refer to a status or position rather than an action or even obedience. A follower of Christ is to walk after the call of Jesus (Luke 9:23). Therefore, naturally, we become more like Him. The Holy Spirit, *parakletos* (John 14:16), transforms our desires to godly desires (Rom. 12:1–2) from the inside out (2 Pet. 3:18).

A transformed life is an attractive life (Acts 9:1–31), but it is not an easy life (John 16:33). Paul said, "I feel as if I'm going through labor pains for you again, and they will continue until Christ is fully developed in your lives" (Gal. 4:19–20 NLT). This transformation Paul mentions is an act of sacrifice (Rom. 12:2). Placing ourselves at the altar of continual dying (Gal. 2:20) will lead our hearts and minds to transformational holy living (1 Pet. 1:15). In his letters to the Corinthians, Paul said, "And the Lord—who is the Spirit—makes us more and more like him as we are changed into his glorious image" (2 Cor. 3:18). Therefore, true disciples are those who not only come to Christ, but those who continually come and follow.

This radical transformation at times could be misunderstood as a one-time, been-there-done-that event (John 3:5) because faith has been taught as an agreement to a set of beliefs rather than obedience to Christ.[5] The Spirit's work in the lives of believers is much more than a dramatic event or a one-time experience (1 Cor. 6:11). The Spirit of God works in each and every believer's life in a continual, progressive manner (Gal. 5:17).

The Greek word πίστις (*pistis*), generally rendered faith or belief, has much to do with allegiance (Rom. 6:20).[6] Faith alone justifies, but it is only the kind of faith that inevitably produces good works

(James 2:17). In the scriptures, you simply cannot find an example of real faith that does not show itself in works. James repeatedly argues that faith without works doesn't save on the last day (James 2:14–26). And faith without works is dead and useless (James 2:17, 20, 26).

Christians are saved by faith alone, but faith that saves alone does not remain alone.[7] Real faith is not passive but active. Intellectual faith without deeds is an empty claim. Ultimately, a mature disciple is one who makes disciples and then teaches students-followers to teach others as well. Only the believers are obedient, and only the obedient believe.[8] I will even say that if you're not changed by grace, you're probably not saved by grace.[9] We have no room for some people to emphasize faith while others stress deeds. You can't have one without the other.

Today, we have cheapened what it means to know Jesus by linking belief to a formulaic prayer that magically imports us into a relationship with God. Get them to pray a little prayer, and people are completely satisfied with themselves. Carnal Christians love to hear that their sins are forgiven. This is ultimately the death of discipleship. They might say, "Well, my status with Jesus is settled. I'm His child. I got the ticket, and I'm going to spend eternity in heaven." In that case, maybe churches ought to call themselves soterian rather than evangelical (that is where we get the word *gospel*), since pastors want only the status term.

Evangelicals cannot give in to the notion of a disagreement about the evangel, about the good news (the gospel), and about the basic foundational definition of what it means to be an evangelical Christian. We were not called to a forgiveness-only gospel but rather to a kingdom gospel. As Bonhoeffer put it, "Justification is

> Today, we have cheapened what it means to know Jesus by linking belief to a formulaic prayer that magically imports us into a relationship with God.

25

the new creation of the new person, and sanctification is the preservation and protection of that person until the day of Jesus Christ."[10] God invites us to come as we are, not stay as we are.

The Reformed (Calvinism) circle often looks at discipleship and says that it sounds like works righteousness and not grace. Or some will say that Christians are not followers of Christ because Paul never referred to Christians as followers. We are more like justified, sanctified, and glorified. The Apostle Paul clearly emphasizes that one becomes a Christian by faith and not by works of the law (Rom. 3:27–28, Eph. 2:8–10). Justification (Rom. 5:9) is a key aspect of the gospel, but the weakness of the transactional model is that the gospel is preached without ongoing transformation. We must unite the theological categories of justification and sanctification by more commonly speaking about the concept of discipleship. Christ's intention for His progressive work throughout our earthly lives is in Christ (Eph. 1:11), through Christ (Eph. 1:15), and through conformity "to the image of his Son, in order that he might be the first born among many" (Rom. 8:29). Sanctification does not provide our justification, although our sanctification proves our justification.

I am certainly not questioning Luther's stand in the 95 theses of grace, *sola gratia* (Latin: grace alone). I celebrate the fact that as evangelicals, we remember the 500th year of Protestant Reformation with Martin Luther, which has influenced Protestants since the sixteenth century. That pivotal moment in 1517 has transformed the world's theology and rediscovery of the gospel through an ordinary simple monk named Martin Luther.[11]

R. C. Sproul, theologian, author, pastor, and founder of Ligonier Ministries, said it well: "In many ways, like in the 7th and 8th century BC prophets of Israel, they [the reformers] saw their task as calling the church back, to the original form, original theology of the apostolic church; that they were not trying to create something new, they were not trying to make a 'New-Form' but to 'Re-Form' the call the church to the roots and its origin."[12] We indeed are saved by grace (Eph. 2:8), through faith (Rom. 3:28), in Christ (John 3:36), on the basis of scripture (2 Tim. 3:16–17), so that God may alone receive all the glory (Psalm 115).

John Calvin believed that we are to distinguish justification and sanctification but must never separate them.[13] Historically, with the Protestant Reformation in the middle of the sixteenth century, the Roman Catholic Church and Protestants drew a line and went their separate ways.[14]

The confusion of these two terms has crippled the effectiveness of gospel stewardship in the current model of church governance and in our preaching. The doctrine of *sola fide* (Latin: by faith alone), also known as justification by faith alone, has been the main focus of the conflict between Protestants and the Roman Catholic Church.[15] But going back to Calvin's stand, justification and sanctification are distinct, although they are never to be set apart from each other. As a result, this understanding has led to the existence of a two-tiered Christian population: those who are saved and just waiting for heaven (justification) and those who are serious about their faith (sanctification). The Bible does not speak of sanctification as a second-level experience.[16] We need to reclaim this lost understanding of biblical salvation.

2. The Consumer Gospel

In the twenty-first century, evangelical churches are caught in a lie of building consumer-mentality believers rather than discipleship leaders. Take all the religious goods and services available through Jesus. The consumer gospel puts a low value on God, and the mission is not a high priority. Therefore, other responsibilities trump discipleship. There will be photography ministries, parking-lot ministries, coffee ministries—oh, and by the way, discipleship ministries somewhere that no one really cares about. Discipleship has become an afterthought that people attempt to squeeze in amid an already full, committed life. Discipleship becomes *a* ministry rather than *the* ministry of the church. The work of discipleship is not one thing the church does; it's what the church does.

Self-indulgence marks the culture in general. People are basically uninterested in anything that doesn't accrue to their own benefit.[17] Churches have accommodated them in this thinking and have thus become locations where certain forms of religious entertainment are displayed for people who, in many cases, sit in a dark room and watch the event take place. Here's what they might say: "Hey, welcome to our church! We want you to be part of our awesome church that is better than the church next door. Here's your cup of coffee and a donut. We have a crazy light show, a smoke machine, a cool hipster worship guy up front, and there's only a 20-minute sermon. And FYI, we really won't ask much of you if you join. All we want is that you show up once a week for a one-hour service so we can tell the higher-ups that we had this many people in the building." Then we pat ourselves on the back and feel good about ourselves.

Jesus was perhaps one of the most seeker-friendly people on Earth, yet I don't think He tried to attract people with a song and a dance. He didn't water down the gospel by saying give me just one hour a month. Instead, He said it is all or nothing. Jesus said on many different occasions, unless you deny yourself (Luke 9:23), sell all your possessions (Matt. 19:21), give up everything (Luke 18:24), and renounce all things (Luke 14:33), you're not worthy to be my disciple (Matt. 10:38).

> Jesus was perhaps one of the most seeker-friendly people on Earth, yet I don't think He tried to attract people with a song and a dance.

The contemporary church movement is the idea that church has become a kind of a spectator sport where you go to watch what happens. Churches are heavily staffed with paid professionals financed by the spectators. Very little and sometimes nothing is asked of those people except occasionally to give some money so the system can continue production. The church has been culturally conditioned and blinded as Christians have been processed and indoctrinated by a secular society that is narcissistic, self-absorbed, and self-centered.

C. S. Lewis, theologian, lecturer, and Christian apologist, predicted this 70 years ago in his book *The Screwtape Letters*. The story takes the form of a series of letters from a senior demon, Screwtape, to his nephew, Wormwood, a junior tempter. The uncle's mentorship pertains to the nephew's responsibility in securing the damnation of a British man known only as the patient. Here is one of Screwtape's encouragements to Wormwood: "There is no need to despair; hundreds of these adult converts have been reclaimed after a brief sojourn in the Enemy's camp and are now with us. All the *habits* of the patient, both mental and bodily, are still in our favour."[18]

If the only thing we have when we leave a Bible study is more head knowledge and spiritual to-do lists for the week, we've missed the point. Christianity detached from mission leads to either lifeless moralism or joyless legalism.

I am persuaded that the church today has many more consumers than committed participants. Our tendency toward ecclesiastical consumerism has seriously weakened the church. For most of us, the church is merely an event we attend or an organization we belong to. The passive culture of the modern evangelical church must be forsaken for the ministry model God has so wisely ordained.

This is the kind of culture we have—a couch-potato culture on the one hand and a fitness culture on the other. In both cases, the idea is to give away your life to satisfy yourself rather than someone else. These kinds of disciples are nearly useless to Christ and His work. We have a bunch of spiritually obese Christians who need to go out and begin to make disciples. As missiologist Alan Hirsch once said, "12 > 12,000. In other words, you can do more with twelve disciples than with twelve thousand religious consumers."[19]

How can we keep the program going? How can we keep the crowds coming? Those are not the things Jesus is most concerned about. All Jesus wanted was a few men who would think as He did, love as He did, see as He did, teach as He did, and serve as He did. All He needed was to revolutionize the hearts of a few, and they would impact the world.[20]

3. The Kingdom Gospel

When people speak about the gospel, it is often referred to as the afterlife, but not so much of how the gospel affects our everyday lives.[21] In order to share Jesus confidently and consistently with others, first share Him confidently and consistently with yourself. If you are not living in such confidence and consistency, you are believing a false gospel. The true, biblical Christianity (the gospel) you believe determines the kind of disciple you become. Believe a false gospel, become a false disciple (Matt. 5:20, 7:21–23, 13:20–21, 18:32–35, 22:10–14).

"The time is fulfilled, and the kingdom of God is at hand; repent and believe in the gospel" (Mark 1:15). If there is a kingdom, then there is a king. If there is a king, then our lives will no longer be the same because the king reigns in that kingdom.[22] Therefore, the gospel is the story of King Jesus, God's son who came, died, and rose again for sinners so that all who believe, repent, and follow Him may inherit the eternal joy in Christ for the kingdom (Mark 1:15, 1 John 4:15, John 1:14, Rom. 10:9–10, John 3:16, 1 Cor. 15:1–5).

In the Gospel of Matthew, an overarching theme is Jesus as the awaited king. He came as a fulfillment of prophecy, born in Bethlehem (Mic. 5:2). Christ fulfilled the Old Testament many times as the son of David (2 Sam. 7:12–13, Matt. 1:1, 12:23, 15:22, 21:9).

Matthew, who was writing to the Jewish people, referred to 45 Old Testament passages. More than half of these references are found only in the Gospel of Matthew. He had a unique way of referring to the Old Testament—that something was "fulfilled." Matthew said it five times in his Gospel (Matt. 1:22–23; 2:15, 17–18; 4:14–16; 8:17). He refers to the son of David nine times. Luke refers to it two times (Luke 18:38, 20:41–21:4), Mark two times (Mark 10:48, 12:35), and John once (John 7:42). This is very important to a Jewish audience. David, the greatest king of Israel, came through Abraham, the first in the Jewish genealogy (Matt. 1:1–17). David was 14th in the genealogy of Abraham.

Jesus repeatedly uses the phrase "kingdom of heaven" (Matt. 16:19, 18:3, 19:23). There has been a debate among scholars for centuries on how to understand the use of "kingdom of heaven" in Matthew. In other books of the Bible, we see "kingdom of God" (Mark 9:1, Luke 4:43; 8:1; 9:2, 27; 10:9; 11:20; 13:18–19; 16:16; 17:20–21; 22:18; 23:51). Jewish people avoided using the word יהוה(Θεός: theos). We never see that in the book of Matthew, which points to that perspective. According to the book of Matthew, the mission of Jesus was first to the Jewish people. When Jesus sent out the 12 disciples, He said, "Go nowhere among the Gentiles" (Matt. 10:5). Jesus came for the Jewish people; therefore, the gospel is famously known as the gospel for the Jews. The apostle Paul mentions "the power of God for salvation to everyone who believes, to the Jew first and also to the Greek" (Rom. 1:16). Jesus is the savior of the Jewish people by fulfilling the Old Testament prophecies from His birth (Matt. 1:22–23).

In Matthew 15, we see Jesus withdrawing from the crowds. We also see the Canaanite woman addressing Jesus as "O Lord, Son of David" (Matt. 15:21–22). As we progress through the book of Matthew, Jesus's kingdom was crucial to the Jews. But Christ prepared the disciples not only for His crucifixion but also for His ascension (Acts 1:6–11). Jesus as the king of heaven plays a huge role in discipleship. We don't think of that very often. People speak of Jesus as a humble servant, but we must also recognize Him as king. Jesus had a universal outlook: "The harvest is plentiful, but the laborers are few" (Matt. 9:37). The field is the world (Matt. 13:1–9). Therefore, the Gospel of Matthew culminates with the Great Commission (Matt. 28:19–20). There is a clear, universal outlook (Matt. 12:18–21, 24:14, 25:32, 26:13).

The end result is that the disciple becomes the kind of person who naturally does what Jesus did.[23] Therefore, Jesus Christ said that in light of the kingdom of God, repentance is giving proper allegiance to King Jesus. The kingdom gospel calls us to abandon our lives and live and walk in Christ-likeness as our identity (2 Cor. 5:17). There must be a willingness to die to self and live for Christ (Gal. 2:20). It is not about you (Rom. 8:9). It is about Him working in and through you (Rom. 11:36). If you are not living that way, you are believing a false gospel (Gal. 1:8–9).

Discipleship, therefore, is not ultimately motivated by strategy but by adoration for King Jesus (John 9:38). As we adore and worship Christ, we must become intentional about making not only disciples who make disciples but also disciples who are able to engage the culture. The kingdom gospel calls us to discipleship (John 8:31–32). The kingdom of God is not a spectator sport. Making disciples is simply the supernatural overflow of being a disciple.

The kingdom gospel is primarily about what God has done to save us and how, when we can receive it through faith, it can only be expressed through our repentance and following (Rom. 2:4). Salvation is spiritual transformation (Rom. 12:2), which is difficult for people with elitist attitudes. Therefore, salvation is people being saved from God, saved by God, and saved for God (Rom 9:1–24).

> Most people want Jesus as a consultant rather than a king (Rev. 19:16). Many want to consume the kingdom of God without first carrying the cross of Christ (Matt 16:24–26).

Most people want Jesus as a consultant rather than a king (Rev. 19:16). Many want to consume the kingdom of God without first carrying the cross of Christ (Matt 16:24–26). The intentional church creates a culture that drives people to the kingdom of God and sends people on the mission (Mark 16:15, Acts 13:47).

We Need to Preach the Gospel to Ourselves Every Day

The gospel has not only been lost in American culture, but it has also lost meaning in churches. We turn to the effects of the gospel—moral change and behavioral modification—but have lost the essence of the gospel. Jesus died the death you and I deserve, conquered the enemy—sin and death. God loves you so much that He sent his son so that whoever believes in Him would never perish but have everlasting life. The gospel begins with God's love, penetrates through the cross and the empty tomb, and results in eternal life for those who believe, which is the reality of the gospel.

However, God doesn't just love you. He loves the world so much that He gave His only son. There are a whole lot of people—people who live right around you—who do not know there is a God who loves them. Therefore, this gospel mission is not our own, and this gospel authority is not ours to keep. All that you and I are called to do is humbly obey and share.

One of the most fundamental marks of an effective church is a church centered on the preaching of the kingdom gospel. In order to do this, we need to understand the right kind of gospel. That reminds me of something Martin Luther said that Jerry Bridges has recently popularized: "We need to preach the gospel to ourselves every day."[24]

It is extremely important that ministry leaders have a compelling, concise, and crystal-clear definition of what the gospel is. Unfortunately, most pastors and ministry leaders have a fuzzy understanding of the gospel. A clear understanding of the gospel compels and causes reproduction and multiplication. Charles Spurgeon said, "I do not think the devil cares how many churches you build, if only you have lukewarm preachers and lukewarm people in them."[25] How can we avoid being lukewarm? By understanding the gospel. If a church leader has a fuzzy understanding of the gospel, the congregation will, too.

The Health of the Church Is the Hermeneutics of the Gospel

The solution is not necessarily to swing the pendulum the other way. We're coming back to the root definition and understanding of the gospel. Discipleship is derived from the gospel, not divorced from the gospel. Why is it important? If a church teaches a skewed, unbiblical version of the gospel, it will discourage genuine Christians and wrongly assure false Christians.

The contemporary gospel is an American cultural artifact. You can become a Christian and not follow Jesus. Discipleship is optional. With a perverse gospel, most discipleship programs do not replicate and ultimately die out. A genuine discipleship in the church context is very much like the discipleship Jesus modeled for us. It is a congregation of men and women who believe the gospel and live by it. Therefore, the health of the church is the hermeneutics of the gospel. A healthy church is how the gospel takes on flesh today.

Where Are We Headed?

Chapter 3

The Jesus Way

We have taken the message of Jesus, but completely
ignored his method, so we have not seen the mission of
Jesus accomplished within His churches.

—Eugene Peterson

It was God's original design from creation in the garden for us
to "be fruitful and multiply" (Gen. 1:28) as image-bearers here on
Earth. God's mission for the church is to advance His kingdom
through discipleship (Matt. 16:19). He has commanded us to make
disciples of all nations, disciples who will obey everything He commanded (Luke 14:25–33).

Part of the problem is that we disciple the way we've been discipled, and the sad reality is that the majority of church leaders
really haven't ever been discipled—at least not intentionally. We are
more accidental disciples. In order to develop disciples, we need to
intentionally train up leaders who understand that discipleship is
more about direction than distinction.[1]

Jesus sees discipleship as an invitation to choose a direction:
"Follow me" (John 21:19). It was not a command to adopt a doctrinal manifesto. Discipleship, by definition, is an ongoing model,
running the race with perseverance (1 Cor. 9:24).

Jesus Applies for Men's Ministry Position

Let's say that your church is looking for a men's ministry director, and Jesus applies. The head of the search committee asks, "Jesus, it seems like you're quite educated and well experienced. Tell us a little a bit about how you will execute your men's ministry here at our church."

Jesus responds, "Well, my plan is to find 12 men and do an intensive, three-year, life-on-life discipleship. By this, I will win the world."

Astonished and frazzled by this answer, the head of the search committee responds, "Well, no way, sir. We need some immediate results. We need bigger numbers right now. Your plan would take too much time and wouldn't look good to our congregation. We cannot offer this position to you."

I say this with tongue in cheek, but Jesus probably wouldn't get a position at any church today if He were to apply. We don't want to do church the way Jesus modeled it in the Bible.

The Jesus Way Is a Countercultural Model

Discipleship takes time. Sadly, as we've seen, churches don't want the Jesus way. Some churches believe they have accomplished the task of discipleship by providing Sunday school classes before their morning services. Then here is the follow-up question: "Great! Then who are the second or third generations in your group?"

Churches want the easy way out. Jesus spent life-on-life with his disciples 24/7, 365 days per year; yet churches instead offer a four-week sermon series and a certificate for finishing a program. This is a huge, problematic issue. Disciples cannot be mass-produced on an assembly line of a conveyor-belt mentality.

Fast-paced church growth is too often rooted in a fleshly desire rather than kingdom advancement. Church leaders, our goal should not be to build a megachurch. Our goal should be to build a healthy church with mature believers.[2] God is unimpressed with human speed. Go deep, not just wide. Grow members, not just numbers. Serve your successor, not just yourself.

The Typical Responses from the Church

Wait! So was the Great Commission given to the pastoral staff, elder board, and trustees? Or was it given to the believers of the local church? Perhaps we already know the answer. Francis Chan in his book *Crazy Love* puts it this way: "We reduce discipleship to a canned program, and so many in the church end up sidelined in a spectator mentality that delegates discipleship to pastors and professionals, ministers and missionaries."[3] Only some Christians will be pastors or missionaries, but all must be disciple-makers. It is not only the paid professionals' task to raise believers, but it is the body of Christ to engage in discipleship. Discipleship cannot be by the few, for the few as an afterthought of the devout and devoted. It is a call of all the saints for all the people to engage in the kingdom advancement for the furtherance of the gospel.

They say it takes a village to raise a child. The Bible shows us it takes a church to grow a Christian. The discipleship models taught in seminaries are pastor-driven rather than embraced by lay people to disciple the body. Discipleship is the cooperative work of God through the body of Christ (Phil. 2:12–13) by pointing and walking with Christ in greater Christ-like maturity. Discipleship begins

> Discipleship cannot be by the few, for the few as an afterthought of the devout and devoted.

with the convicting ministry of the Holy Spirit (Gal. 5:16–23) by the revealing ministry of the holy scripture (John 17:17) through the interceding ministry of God's holy son (1 Pet. 2:22) and for the eternal ministry of the holy father (1 Cor. 8:6).

Discipleship—that's the job of the pastor. We may never say it out-wardly, but subconsciously, we assume that discipleship is only for ecclesiastical professionals. We live in a society that has been taught that pastors, elders, and deacons do all the work of the ministry, although Paul said "to equip the saints for the work of ministry" (Eph. 4:12).

Most pastors visit people in the hospital, officiate at weddings, and become funeral directors of dying congregations. All these are important and crucial, but the reality is that those environments fail to encourage people into a life of discipleship. The ministry of the church is for all who are called to share in Christ's life. Yes, it is easier and more comfortable to rely on pastors to do the ministry of the Great Commission. But the pastorate is for those who possess the peculiar gift of being able to help other men and women practice any ministry to which they are called.

I often hear people say, "Well, God can't use me; I'm just an everyday normal guy. I'm not in the ordained clergy circle." Let's see what the book of Acts says: "Now when they saw the boldness of Peter and John, and perceived that they were uneducated, common men, they were astonished. And they recognized that they had been with Jesus" (Acts 4:13).

We forget that God has used mere ordinary, uneducated people to turn the world upside down. In the Gospel accounts, Jesus's earthly ministry was with 12 disciples, ordinary men with many weaknesses. Jesus chose these real nobodies—fishermen, tax collec-tors, political zealots—and turned their weaknesses into strengths, producing greatness from the mundane. Peter had a big prob-lem with his mouth and was a bundle of contradictions (Matt. 16:21–23). Andrew, Peter's brother, was quiet and stayed behind the scenes. James and John, the so-called Sons of Thunder, were aggressive, hot-headed, ambitious, and intolerant (Mark 3:17). Philip was skeptical and negative; he had limited vision. *We can't do that* summed up his faith when confronted with feeding the five thousand (John 6:5–7). Nathaniel (Bartholomew) was prejudiced and opinionated. Matthew was the most hated person in Capernaum, working in a profession that abused innocent people (Matt. 9:9–13). Thomas was melancholy, mildly depressed, and pessimistic (John 20:24–29). James, the son of Alphaeus, and Judas, the son of James, were nobodies. The Bible says nothing about them. Simon the Zealot was a freedom fighter and terrorist in his day (Matt. 10:4). Judas the treasurer was a thief and a loner. He pretended to be loyal to Jesus before finally betraying Him (Matt. 26:14–16). When you feel unqualified to be used by God, remember this: He tends to recruit from the pit, not the pedestal. If God can use people such as these 12 men, He can use you and me to make disciples.

I used to think you had to be special in order for God to use you, but now I know you simply need to say yes. Our greatest challenge isn't finding talented leaders or raising money; it is finding ourselves. It is often our selfish desire to control our lives and our unwillingness to let go of our insecurity that prevent multiplication. Some of us may need a little heart check. Paul says, "But God chose what is foolish in the world to shame the wise; God chose what is weak in the world to shame the strong; God chose what is low and despised in the world, even things that are not, to bring to nothing things that are" (1 Cor. 1:27–28).

> I used to think you had to be special in order for God to use you, but now I know you simply need to say yes.

The word *disciple* in the New Testament does not mean a second-stage Christian. Too many people too often assume that discipleship belongs to the elite, noble people who know all the right Sunday school answers. Some ministries build on this idea, which is unbiblical.

> The word *disciple* in the New Testament does not mean a second-stage Christian. Too many people too often assume that discipleship belongs to the elite, noble people who know all the right Sunday school answers.

There is nothing new under the sun (Eccles. 1:9). This is the same old lie that even the religious leaders were deceived by and caught up in. In Luke 15, we witness the first trash-talk by religious leaders. In Luke 15:1–2, as people were listening to what Jesus was saying, the Pharisees said, "This man receives sinners and eats with them." Yes, Jesus came for sinners, something the Pharisees never expected. They were grumbling and fighting under their breath.

Discipleship is for all of us—people who messed up, people who don't have their acts together, people who are dealing with problems. Contrary to what some churches do, Jesus didn't avoid people who mess up. He ran to them.[4] Jesus came for the pimps, prostitutes, and messed up sinners. And He didn't just come for them; He chose these nobodies by empowering them regardless of color, race, background, creed, or socioeconomic status. With the spirit of God, they can wield the word of God for the ministry of God for the glory of God—to change the world.

Followers of Jesus are called to be Christ's ambassadors (2 Cor. 5:20) (Greek: *ekklesia*, called-out-ones [1 Pet. 2:9]), sent out (John 3:34) in order to impact the world for His glory (Rom. 11:36). How can these two truths (ordinary and radical) collide and work together?

The Problem with Radicalism

The etymology of the term *radical* (Latin root: radix) is the best reason not to concede it to nostalgia. Radical discipleship is about nothing more and nothing less than laying bare the roots of the gospel. However, in today's context, radical is an offensive term since it is associated with terrorist groups.

Jesus will never ask His disciples to strap on a bomb and detonate it in the middle of a shopping mall. You want to be radical? Jesus says, "For even the Son of Man came not to be served but to serve, and to give his life as a ransom for many" (Mark 10:45). Jesus served even those who hated Him so completely that He allowed them to hang Him on a cross. Try to serve someone who hates you to the point that they will murder you. There's nothing more radical than laying your life down for the sake of someone else. If you want to be distinct, love someone who disdains you. If you want to be extraordinary, serve someone who discourages you. If you want to be radical, pray with someone who despises you. In this context, *radical* means "Jesus with flesh on" (John 1:14) so you can give a word, a look, a touch in the name of Jesus.

Jesus's Ongoing Ministry with His Disciples

While churches are looking for decisions, Jesus is looking for disciples. Making disciples initially requires evangelism (Mark 16:15), but it doesn't end there (Acts 1:8). Discipleship cannot end with evangelism because making disciples is an ongoing relationship. Shifting from giving a gospel presentation to having a gospel conversation takes pressure off the witness and relates the gospel more clearly to an unbeliever.[5]

You don't meet a lot of people who say, "Prove the gospel to me." You actually meet a lot of people who say, "Can you live it? How does this connect to my everyday life?" There is a sense that the more we know somebody, the more our words don't matter as much as our life. People must see our changed lives as much as they hear the message from us. One living demonstration of the gospel is far better than a hundred explanations of many sermons. It is good to tell people what we mean, but it is way better to show them.[6]

We Love Jesus's Truth, not Jesus's Way

"I am the way, and the truth, and the life," said Jesus (John 14:6). We evangelicals have been faithfully preaching Jesus's truth—salvation by grace through faith in Christ alone. But when it comes to Jesus's way of disciple-

> In essence, we've taken the message of Jesus but completely ignored His method, so we haven't seen the mission of Jesus accomplished on Earth.

ship, we aren't so faithful. Therefore, we don't see Jesus's life in the church—no vibrancy, passion, zeal, or excitement for the gospel. In essence, we've taken the message of Jesus but completely ignored His method, so we haven't seen the mission of Jesus accomplished on Earth.

Are You Walking in the Footsteps of Christ?

If we want to walk in Christ's footsteps, we begin to do what He intended for us in the first place. Paul said, "Be imitators of me, as I am of Christ" (1 Cor. 11:1). The Greek word is μιμηταί, imitators of me, from which we get the English word *mimic*. Another translation says, "Follow my example, as I follow the example of Christ" (1 Cor. 11:1 NIV). Paul is commanding the believers in Corinth to follow his example, as he follows Christ's. Christ's example is that He "did not please himself" (Rom. 15:1–3). Paul encouraged the Corinthians to remember Christ's great sacrifice as the perfect model of love and concern for others (Heb. 10:1–18). Christ gave up His freedom and honor, humbling Himself to the point of death on a cross in order to save others (Phil. 2:5–8).

The word *Christian* does not mean one who admires Christ or one who is the recipient of Christ's blessings. It is not even one who believes in Christ. By definition, Christian means a follower of Christ. Those who aren't following Jesus aren't His followers. It's that simple.

Followers follow, and those who don't follow aren't followers. To follow Jesus means to take up His dream and work for it. It is better to simply admit that people who live like non-Christians are likely non-Christians.

The Opportune Moment to Let Love Shine

We find that transformation tends to happen as people become committed in ever-increasing measure to three things: Christ, His church, and His cause. We have found that making these commitments enables the Holy Spirit to transform people more and more into extraordinary followers of Christ.

While the harvest is plentiful, the workers are few (Matt. 9:37). There has never been a more crucial moment than now. Now is the opportune time for gospel outreach to the broken, needy, and perishing sinners, for Christ's glory. In the midst of a darkness overwhelming our society, now is the opportunity for the church to shine even brighter. When sin abounds, the gospel abounds even more (Rom. 5:20).

Mark Dever said, "The motive for discipling others begins in the love of God and nothing less. He has loved us in Christ, and so we love him. And we do this in part by loving those he has placed around us."[7] If we work together with a heart of submission and compassion, we will be able to love one another.

Chapter 4

The Local Church

We must build bridges of *relationship* strong enough
to bear the *weight* of the *truth we have to give.*

—Reggie Joiner

As a pastor of a local church in Missouri, I remember the advice I first received when I entered full-time ministry. A pastor from another church approached me and said, "Well, you got to remember one thing: don't become friends with those you minister to. Staffs are employees, and you just want to keep a professional relationship." This left me in a dilemma. Although his advice made practical sense, I couldn't reconcile what he said with the Bible's call to "love one another" (John 13:34). As renowned author C. S. Lewis once wrote, "To love at all is to be vulnerable."[1] And this, Lewis suggests, means giving your heart to others at the expense of it being wronged and possibly broken. Unfortunately, as my friend's comment showed, vulnerability, or love, for that matter, doesn't seem to be a priority in the church—and that, I believe, is extremely worrisome.

We need a generation who will be willing to stand in the gap, a generation that will go countercultural in loving confrontation, making discipleship an automatic mentality for authentic relationships.[2]

From my experience since entering full-time ministry, here are some lessons I've learned on the need for vulnerability in the body of Christ.

The Dispute and Debate about Discipleship

I often hear a debate on the right way of discipleship. Rather than arguing the semantics over discipleship and how to approach it, I think we should just simply do it and begin to live in a different light. Something has to change. We've argued too long while thousands of people have passed by our eyes.

Discipleship is the people. We are in the people business at church. People cannot grow in their faith when they're not in an environment where they can be discipled.

> I often hear a debate on the right way of discipleship. Rather than arguing the semantics over discipleship and how to approach it, I think we should just simply do it and begin to live in a different light.

Jesus Became Vulnerable for Us

The creator of the universe looked upon guilty, needy, perishing sinners and was moved by compassion.[3] So out of love for us (John 3:16), He sent His only begotten son, Jesus Christ, into this world (John 1:14).

Though He could have chosen to come as a high, mighty, and distant king, Jesus instead chose to become vulnerable like each one of us, tempted in every way, and able to empathize with our weaknesses (Heb. 4:15–16). He counted Himself as nothing, humbled Himself, and came to serve in the lowest of places (Mark 10:45, John 6:38, Phil. 2:8). And 1 John 4:9 tells exactly why Jesus did all this: because of His love for us. But it doesn't stop there. Just as God loved us, we are called to love one another (1 John 4:11).

But as followers of Jesus, we seem to accept Jesus's love for us but ignore His call to love one another. If we fail to experience Jesus's life of passion and zeal for the church, could it be because we have not followed His ways in loving others, mainly because we fear the messiness and trouble it brings us?

Jesus Just Did Life

In Jesus's model of discipleship, we don't see Him constantly inviting people to the synagogues to hear the rabbi preach or teach that weekend. We see Him selecting His disciples and saying, "Follow me" (Mark 1:17). Jesus didn't even say, "Show up to class and listen to me teach." He said to come and follow Him. Having called his men, He made it His practice to just be with them. That was the essence of His training program—letting His disciples follow Him. Jesus was the guide to a group of disciples on a daily basis and lived life with them. True discipleship teaches us to live out our faith in community. The reason discipleship works in the church is that it empowers the church to be the church rather than a building.

In Acts 2:42, the word κοινωνία (Greek: *koinonia*, fellowship) is more the idea of shared space, but it is an environment where people begin to say, "Your burden is my burden, your joy is my joy, and your life is my life." As we look to the life of Christ, rarely do we see radical disciples birthed out of participation in a one-hour Sunday morning worship service. Radical discipleship takes place in a relational environment where people feel comfortable exploring their personal and spiritual issues and learning what it means to be a follower of Jesus.

> Jesus didn't even say, "Show up to class and listen to me teach." He said to come and follow Him.

The Transforming Power of Transparency

Having worked as a youth pastor, I've noticed one thing. Young people are able to read between the lines fairly quickly. They can see past the structure and programs to whether you truly care about them as individuals. Sadly, it's not uncommon to hear comments from young people such as this: "Well, the church was judgmental and hypocritical. I don't want to be part of that" or "I just didn't feel connected to the people at my church."

Just a month ago, one of our core leaders in the church told me that I couldn't be vulnerable and share my past because it would get people worried that their leader didn't have his life together. But isn't that the actual reality? We all don't have our lives together. The truth is that I am just a needy, guilty, and wretched sinner who is saved by a merciful, heavenly father. There is really no such thing as mighty men of God, but only weak, pitiful, and faithless people of a great and mighty God.

In fact, it is when we are vulnerable enough to say, "I don't have my act together; I need Jesus" that God shows His strength in us (2 Cor. 12:9–11). It all points to Christ. It's all about Him and His grace. We need to be vulnerable for the sake of the gospel. We need to understand that the gospel of Christ is about embracing lost sinners and growing together in a vibrant community.

The Great Commandment (Matt. 22:37–40)

The members of a local church should cultivate a culture of discipleship because they love their neighbor and care for the next generation. "You shall love the Lord your God with all your heart and with all your soul and with all your mind....You shall love your neighbor as yourself" (Matt. 22:37, 39). Too often, the church is a place where people feel more beaten up about their sins than loved. Jesus always goes for conversation and conviction rather than condemnation and coercion. What if the church were a city of refuge that people ran to rather than ran from?

Christ-like love is an attractive love. Sometimes people want to immediately kick off with some sort of strategy for reaching the lost, but apart from love, we are nothing but a clanging cymbal to God (1 Cor. 13:1). You may be saying, "Yeah, yeah, I know Jesus is love, so we love people." However, the world has somewhat figured out that Christians are a whole lot better at the talk than the walk, and then they turn their backs on it.

Great Commission > Great Commandment?

I was recently in a meeting with a few members of the church who asked this question: "How are we known in our community?" In the book *The Neighboring Church*, one of the authors, Rich Rusaw, asks a fundamental question that churches have been too scared to ask. "If my church ceased to exist today, would anyone notice we were gone? Would anyone even care to know? Would anyone notice the church was gone since the body of Christ has been so active in the community loving Jesus?"[4] I took it a step further. If my church ceased to exist today, would the community be impacted by its lack of presence because we loved our neighbors so well?

But the real question is actually within ourselves. If I were to cease to exist in the community, would my neighbors notice that my family and I weren't there anymore?

This is a hard diagnostic question to ask. It's easy for me to control my own personal perception of the impression I would leave, but I cannot necessarily control how others in the community see me.

Part of the issue here is that the church has forgotten the task of the Great Commandment in favor of the Great Commission. The Great Commission without the Great Commandment grieves the heart of God (Psalms 78:40). As Rick Warren said, "A Great

Commitment to the Great Commandment and the Great Commission will grow a Great Church."[5]

In other words, people can tell if your Great Commission is greater than your Great Commandment. For example, if we go with the old traditional model of operating a church, we are subconsciously saying, "We want to pack the pews every Sunday. We are glad you're here, but we're not really interested in having you here because we are interested in your friend back there more." What happens as a result is that people don't feel cared for, so they leave.

The Difficulty in Disciple-Making

Today, with technological advancements and social media, if we don't want to deal with someone, we simply delete them from our friends list, log off our Twitter account, and move on with our life. That doesn't happen with real-life people. If we don't have empathy, we mentally check out and go about our own lives, forgetting that there are real people dealing with real struggles that are crushing their souls.

Jesus could have wired the universe with a stereo on Mars, woofers and tweeters on Jupiter, and the angel choir singing to us about the gospel. But instead, "the Word became flesh and dwelt among us" (John. 1:14). Isn't it ironic? In an age when methods of rapid communication of the gospel are available to the church, there are actually more unevangelized people on the Earth today than before the invention of the horseless carriage.

Part of the problem is that our hearts are not broken for the things that break God's heart. Empathy is a natural consequence of compassion (Matt. 9:1–8). Jesus was never divorced from His compassion (Matt. 9:18–34). When we look to Christ, who was fully God yet fully man (Heb. 2:5–18), we will begin to develop a heart that is ruled by the peace of God (Phil. 4:7). The world will begin to see the depth of sympathy and empathy stemming from Christ's love in us, born of a relationship with Him (2 Cor. 1:3–4).

The Role of the Local Church

Too often, people try to accomplish the task of discipleship apart from the local church. I believe this is impossible because God's work of personal transformation is intended to take place within the community of God's people. Discipleship doesn't happen apart from the context of the local church because God has chosen the local church as His instrument to fulfill the Great Commission. There is no such thing as a solo discipleship.

In the book of Ephesians, the apostle Paul says that "through the church the manifold wisdom of God might now be made known to the rulers and authorities in the heavenly places" (Eph. 3:10). Jesus established the apostles (Eph. 2:20) to be the foundation of the church and built it with prophets, teachers, pastors, and ordained men (1 Tim. 3:1–7) so there will be a structure of local churches in the body of Christ that is called the church.

I sense a grave danger of confusion in regard to the doctrine of the church, especially in the nature and function of the church. I will come boldly and say that apart from the body of Christ, discipleship is impossible.[6] This is the way God designed the Christian life—a local church where a group of people, covenanted together, gather regularly for corporate worship (Col. 3:16), the celebration of the ordinances (Luke 22:19), ministering of the word of God (Col. 1:24–29), the leadership of qualified leaders (1 Tim. 3:1–7), and submission to the body on the mission for Christ and the world (Eph. 3:14–21). It is a community that promotes authentic spiritual growth among God's people in ways that are grace-based and gospel-centered, relationally and theologically driven, grounded in the local church.[7]

As Albert Mohler said in light of the local church, "One of the lessons we can learn from the evangelical movement is that its central weakness was not epistemological. Its central weakness was not its commitment to the core doctrines of the Christian faith. Its central weakness was ecclesiological—an undervaluing of the local church in particular."[8]

Biblical Membership Is a Declaration of Citizenship in Christ's Kingdom

What role does the local church play in personal transformation? Can a person grow apart from the local church? A misunderstanding of formal church membership has crippled the effectiveness of the local church in our context.[9]

The church is where the people of God unite for the gospel mission under the biblically prescribed offices that God has ordained. They devote themselves to the apostles' teachings. They share fellowship, the breaking of bread, and prayer.[10] They call themselves believers and share everything in common, including their possessions and goods as people have a need (Acts 2:44–45).

You might be saying, "Well, Jonathan, what about those who have loved Jesus for 30 years but don't like the church and don't attend?" Of the 114 times the church is mentioned in the New Testament, at least 90 of them refer to specific local gatherings of believers who have banded together for fellowship and mission.[11] So statements like these are lies: "I love Jesus, but I don't like the church." "I will never leave Jesus, but I'm done with the church." In a sense, they are saying, "I love Jesus, but I don't submit to his word." The scripture says, "If you love me, you will keep my commandments" (John 14:15).

It is impossible to read this passage of scripture and come away with the idea that Christianity is a just-me-and-Jesus sort of religion. Salvation is something that connects us to God and his people. Just a personal and private commitment is an impossibility. Part of the problem is that we live with this kind of an individualistic idea: "This is how I will spend my time—the way I want it, and you have no say in that." That has tremendously affected how we understand the church in Western civilization.

The biblical recognition of the system God has put in place is always evident in local churches. The life and authority of the local church shape the lives of its members. What we see in scripture is that God forms us in pretty profound ways when we gather to worship. We may not really feel it, but the formation is usually occurring through the ordinary means of gathering together, such as singing together, hearing the word of God together, and breaking bread in communion.

The church is not a meeting you attend or a place you enter. It's an identity that is yours in Christ, an identity that shapes your whole life so life and mission become everything within you.[12]

Local Church as God's Plan of Fostering Biblical Discipleship

When the apostle Paul was discipling new believers, he repeatedly reminded them that there was help in Christ and Christ's people, the church. He said that Christ "has broken down in his flesh the dividing wall of hostility" (Eph. 2:14). We are "fellow citizens with the saints and members of the household of God" (Eph. 2:19). We are "being built together into a dwelling place for God" (Eph. 2:22).

Therefore, the local church is not an option; it is God's primary way for believers to grow in love for Him and love for fellow believers. But believers bypass it. In the New Testament, to be a Christian meant to be saved into the church, baptized into the church, and immediately made part of a covenant community together. We don't see free-agent Christians roaming around the New Testament.

Why is it important? Because it is biblical. Skipping church or not being part of a church is disobedience. Don't neglect this. Make it a priority in your life (Heb. 10:25). Gathering of the saints is crucial and essential to the faith, for the good of your own soul, for the mission of Christ, and for the health of the local congregation.

Mutual Accountability

Mutual accountability is a biblical picture. In order to change this culture of mutual accountability that is theologically rooted, we must first teach it clearly. But in order to teach it clearly, we must understand it well as a church. I believe that begins with proper expositional preaching, biblical theology, church discipleship, and growth within the church.

When these collide, unity forms. In a culture of discipleship, unity is a starting point. Both relationships and spiritual formation happen inside and outside the church context. Relational community through the relational environment is found in this discipleship context.

As believers wrestle together in the local church context through various trials, temptations, tribulations, suffering, and persecution of the faith, they will each draw closer to Christ and to one another and strengthen the bond of faith and unity (1 Pet. 4:12–19).

Characterized by Authenticity

Mutual accountability in a community of believers is characterized by authenticity. The idea of authenticity has recently received a significant amount of attention as people search for meaning in life. Someone perhaps may comment, "Well, this Jesus thing is private to me, so I keep it to myself." Following Jesus may be personal, but it's never private. Instead, we live a life that is marked by our own selfish glory rather than God's glory. We will multiply the gospel only when we allow others to get close enough to us to see the life of Christ in action.

The greatest threat in the Christian circle is the lack of authenticity for committed and efficient leaders. Leaders must not only encourage people to be open and honest but to be models as well. Many things are caught rather than taught. The loss of authenticity in the church is a loss of vital power in the community. Authenticity can be the first step in reviving the effectiveness of the church.

Accountability + Authenticity = Church Discipline

People say they want friendship and community, but if you mention accountability or commitment, they run the other way. Why? Often, there are two reasons: an unhealthy need for privacy and hidden sin.

Then you may hear a response such as this: "We are all part of the body of Christ. We are free to go wherever we want." If you go freely wherever you so desire, you are disconnecting yourself from an accountable relationship with church members (Matt. 18:15–16). Jesus assumes that His disciples will belong to a church. When a disciple is out of step with his brother or sister, a church will be there to love, pursue, and discipline that person under submission (Heb. 13:18).

Therefore, fellowship is the people of God united for the gospel mission under the biblically prescribed offices that God has ordained—offices of those who have devoted themselves to the apostles' teachings. If people put aside Sunday morning and go elsewhere, they are forfeiting God's design for helping them grow spiritually.

Authentic faith and accountability naturally lead to the beauty of church discipline. However, the idea of church discipline is absolutely foreign to our evangelical churches today. The absence of church discipline is no longer remarkable; it is generally not even existent. It is so much more than simply going to church; it is pouring our lives out to one another in the church. To those we love, we will speak the truth in love (Eph. 4:15) and hold them accountable, which is the definition of church discipline (Matt. 18:15–20).

When discipline leaves a church, Christ goes with it. An undisciplined church without mutual accountability characterized by authenticity becomes a weak, flabby, foolish, and unchaste church.[13] Without a proper biblical framework of the church community, we cannot grow to full maturity in Christ. Jesus is interested in the process of progressive sanctification— daily growth in Christ Jesus. God is not interested in the quantity of disciples but rather the quality of discipleship.[14] The goal of a church must be to present to God every Christian "mature in Christ" (Col. 1:28).

Do Life vs. Do Programs

Let's begin by acknowledging that the solution doesn't lie in a program. Discipleship is too often misunderstood as a program (a classroom setting). According to Jesus's example, discipleship is not a program we launch. It is a lifestyle we embrace. Discipleship to Jesus is more obedience than knowledge. While churches are constantly looking for one curriculum, one program, one strategy, and one system, God has laid it out pretty clear in scriptures. The one method is the Great Commission. Programs don't grow people— never have, never will. People grow people. That doesn't mean that programs are bad and that we must toss them out. It means that discipleship is a command, not a program. Mark Dever, the president of 9Marks ministry, said in his book *Discipling: How to Help Others Follow Jesus* that "churches don't need programs so much as they need cultures of discipling, cultures where each member prioritizes the spiritual health of others."[15]

Many church programs fail. Training disciples happens in true relationships with one another. Discipleship is at the center of what it means to be a follower of Christ—to be a disciple who makes disciples. It is the mission of our lives. It defines us. A disciple is a disciple-maker and not something we program. It becomes a lifestyle. Programs are labor-intensive in the beginning, followed by routine maintenance. People require constant work. That is why most people choose programs over people. In fact, I would even say that over-programming is a sign that the church is in its decline. Healthy churches approach discipleship as a path, not a program. Ultimately, discipling involves living out the whole Christian life before others.

Now, don't get me wrong. Programs are not bad; however, programs are tools in your discipleship process. We must first start with the right place. As Eric Geiger, vice president of the Church Resource Division at LifeWay Christian Resources, said, "The biggest mistake ministry leaders make … is to start with their programs. Start with your discipleship process, not with your programs."[16]

I often say to our leaders, "You are the curriculum. What people see in you should have a tremendous impact on their lives." What if we brought this first-century principle into the twenty-first century of living an honest, transparent lifestyle as Jesus did? We need real, authentic, transparent care for one another through a high-grade sense of the gospel.

Chapter 5

The Biblical Blueprint

*Most pastors and church staff understand the need
for and importance of disciple making, but
many don't know where to start.*

—Eric Geiger

Football season brings stories of rags to riches, underdogs to
champions—it's a season of glory. A coach comes into the locker
room and says something like, "We're going to win the game!"
Everyone cheers, and excitement overwhelms the room.

The players run onto the field, get into formation, and then the
game begins. What happens next? Total chaos! No one knows what
the players are trying to do, and they don't know how to score. The
coach calls a time-out, gathers the team around, and says again,
"Men, we are here to win the game!"

What the coach really needed was to teach them *how* to win
the game. Many people in our churches are facing a similar tragedy.
"Go make disciples!" Everyone is all in. However, the church doesn't
seem so sure about how that ought to look, so they get confused and
frustrated and move on to something else. They know what they are
called to do, but there's no plan, so the pastor gets frustrated, and
the flock gets confused.

The helplessness leads to future hopelessness, which causes churchgoers to jump on another bandwagon and repeat the same task over and over again, expecting a different result.

Game Plan for Winning the Game

When I was a young convert, I felt an urgency rush through my mind that we need to share this good news with the whole world. After learning the profound truth of the gospel and the need for it, how could I not share it? The answer I often got from church leaders was, "Yeah, yeah, discipleship is important." But I wasn't sure what they meant. Who would say discipleship isn't important?

Little by little, I began to see these flaws in my own ministry and in the church as a whole. If church leaders have no plan, you can assume they are not interested in practicing discipleship. If you don't know what to do, you don't do anything at all. If you don't have a plan, you don't intend to do it. In fact, if you don't have a plan, you won't ever make it happen. It is hard to think of many things that do more damage to the effectiveness of the church than church leaders who have no plan for making disciples. As a result, it has paralyzed and crippled people in the task of the Great Commission.

Some believers say, "Well, I make disciples. I have Christian friends." But not all relationships where spiritual conversations take place are the discipling kind of relationship. Intentionality is the key. Discipleship requires an intentional effort on the part of one person (a disciple-maker) to impart spiritual principles into the life of another (a disciple). Discipleship is going through the rhythm of life, investing in one person at a time.

Churches need to implement a strategy to accomplish that mission. Because the mission of a local church is to make disciples, a strategy is how the church is designed to make disciples. If a church's strategy is not grounded in making disciples, the church has abandoned the mission Christ has given. That mission includes knowing your end goal or purpose—knowing what a disciple is, recognizing what one looks like, and learning how to make one.

Implication of the Great Commission (Matt. 28:18–20)

In Matthew 28:18–20, Jesus commissioned the 12 disciples to make disciples. In those verses, Matthew represented Jesus as one who has authority. He also stated His authority on Earth to forgive sins (Matt. 9:6) because everything had been handed over to Him by God the father (Matt. 11:27).

Jesus commanded the disciples to go to all the nations. Matthew may have intended Jesus's words to be understood as arranged in a chiasmatic statement around baptism in Matthew 28:19. Balanced around this was discipling (verse 19) and teaching (verse 20). Around these are statements about authority (verse 18) and presence (verse 20).

Not for one moment did Jesus lose sight of His goal. No wasted energy, not an idle word. He was in business for God (Luke 2:49). Jesus's freshly confirmed authority is the basis for His new directive to the disciples. Matthew restricts his use of the noun *disciple* (μαθητής) to the 12 disciples, but by making a wider use of other language markers of discipleship and more pointedly by his wider use of the cognate verb *disciple* (μαθητεύειν), Matthew indicates that the discipleship of the 12, although unique and unrepeatable, embodied patterns of discipleship that are of a more general relevance.

Matthew has used the phrase πάντα τὰ ἔθνη three times already. Whatever the complexity of the actual development, it remains important that the New Testament widely claims the mission to all nations is grounded in a command of the risen Jesus. It is tragically easy for those of us in ministry to forget this, to get so wrapped up in nuances of theology and specific strategies that we no longer personally seek the lost. Disciples are called to triumphantly preach the triumphant Christ of the triumphant gospel to the lost and dying world. Discipleship changes the come-and-see mentality to a go-and-tell one.

Whatever your vocation and location, you are on a mission. We are all on the mission to fulfill the Great Commission. This mission wouldn't be a commission unless we commit to cooperatively participating in that mission. Again, faith is only real if it's in action. Therefore, we have been committed by Christ, for Christ, and through Christ. We must not only make converts but also make disciples who obey Jesus's commands in every way. A disciple is a learner, an apprentice, a repenter of sins, a believer of the good news, a follower of Jesus. According to Dallas Willard, obedience is where the Holy Spirit meets us.[1]

Are We Winning the Game? (Biblical Metrics for Church Success)

What does a win look like as a church? Where are we headed? What are we called to do in the church?[2] Those were the questions I asked my small group at our first meeting after a long summer break. Everyone had different answers. In order to know how to gauge the effectiveness of our churches, we need a rule book to measure church success.

How do you measure the success of discipleship? What are even the biblical metrics for measuring success? Is it church attendance? How often people have devotions? How much money each is giving? The standard of success becomes a numbers game. Many churches and church leaders have fallen into the trap of gauging the church's success by the ABCs of growth: attendance, buildings, and cash. One of the first questions people outside the church ask me is, "How big is your church?" If we stop to think about that question, it's a self-centered, fleshly, earthly question, isn't it? What does the size of the church have to do with the health of the church? As Charles H. Spurgeon said, "Just because a church is large doesn't mean it's healthy. It could just mean it's swollen."[3] It is a repudiation to the theocentric leadership that's driven by secular ideological and anthropocentric leadership. Discipleship has and always will be the war against the kingdom of God versus the kingdom of self. It is so much more than a horizontal problem; it is a vertical problem with God.

In this sense, in New Testament churches, there were no successful churches. How can we keep the program going? How can we keep the crowds coming? Those are *not* the concerns of Jesus. He is not concerned about the programs, crowds, or personalities who fill the senior pastor's shoes. The leaders of the first-century church did not ask each other, "How many came to church last week?" That's not how God measures success.

> Discipleship has and always will be the war against the kingdom of God versus the kingdom of self. It is so much more than a horizontal problem; it is a vertical problem with God.

When we look at the life of Jesus, we see that He didn't draw large crowds for the sake of counting heads or logging attendance. He never gauged effectiveness by nickels and noses. Therefore, the goal of the church should not be to build a megachurch. The end goal is to build a healthy church with mature believers. In discipleship, our focus as a church is not the quantity of disciples but the quality of disciples. If you take care of the depth, God will take care of the width.[4]

The goal for your worship service should never be greater attendance; it's to cultivate a heart of worship and love for God in people's lives. What if we weigh Christians in the church with these five categories: missions, accountability, reproductive, communal, and scriptural?[5]

An effective ministry is not gauged by how many ministries it executes but how well it equips others to partake in ministry (Heb. 13:21). Too often, the focus of most churches is how to survive a little longer. Dr. Shaw, one of my professors, once said, "Leadership development isn't fast, and our tendency is to quit."

Biblical Blueprint for Disciple-Making

Many churches throughout America have no succession plan in place because they've created an environment in which they don't have to. Therefore, nothing is happening. Why would we raise another worship guy if we already have a decent guy? Why would we raise another youth pastor if we already have one?

First, we must clarify the discipleship process. What is the process (the blueprint) of making disciples? Where are we to begin? God is looking for FAT disciples.

- Faithful — Committed to the things of God. The opposite is sporadic, impulsive, and unwilling. If someone is not serious about his or her faith, that person is not ready.
- Available – Allocating time and priority to growing in his or her walk with Christ and in his or her relationships. The opposite is not prioritizing or valuing the importance of time together. It does not work to disciple someone you have to beg or who is too busy to study outside your meeting.
- Teachable – Willing to learn and open to seeing new truths through honest questions. The opposite is proud and argumentative at every turn.

The Four-Leadership Square

After you've gone through the selection process, as Jesus did with the 12 disciples, and found those who are faithful, available, and teachable disciples, you are ready to go. The question then is this: "Now what? I don't know the plan yet." Churches don't need more managers; they need more leaders who have an intentional plan for discipling others. Jesus not only selected his leaders, but He was also a great leader who trained His disciples to be effective leaders. If you want to be the best, you learn from the best. Jesus happens to be the master at making disciples, and he has modeled it according to the scriptures.[6]

Rather than making disciples, churches seem to be looking for disciples. Church leaders feel the need for disciples in the ministry and tend to say, "I need a person to fill the children's ministry. Let me go find a disciple."

Announcements may go like this: "We are in desperate need of leaders in the children's area. If you don't serve, the whole ministry will fall apart." Then come more reactionary and guilt-trip tactics, and people pray. Some will think, "Well, the Spirit of God is telling me to do it. I need to obey Jesus." Churches then find these brand-new leaders and throw them into the deep end of the pool—baptism by fire in the name of Jesus. No wonder the majority of people who serve in any leadership position say,

> We cannot microwave disciples; they are a crock pot recipe.

"Well, I'm never doing that again!" They burn out and move on. Those who are church leaders today sadly are those who survived the leadership-dumping crisis.

The current leadership development plan is this: "Oh, you have a passion and desire to lead? There you go! Here's the curriculum, and this is the room and hour you will teach. Go figure it out, and I won't be with you in the midst of it all." They commission people in the wilderness of the unknown and call it oversight.

Too many churches want leadership development to be fast and easy, but in reality it's not. We cannot microwave disciples;

they are a crock pot recipe. Church leaders can create instead a pipeline of a process that leadership can walk through and that is a reproducible.[7] Even secular academic internship programs do an excellent job of this.

1. I Do. You Watch. An experienced leader wouldn't allow a new teaching intern straight out of college to teach on the first day of class. An apprentice needs a lot of direction and investment because he or she has little experience and low competency. Jesus spent the majority of this time as a servant leader observing and watching (debriefing) as he intentionally trained His disciples (Luke 5:27–28).

2. I Do. You Help. In this phase, we see Jesus giving the disciples responsibility such as feeding 5,000 people on a mountain and allowing them to partake in the ministry (Matt. 14:13–21). Jesus showed grace and vision in this stage of development. This stage is often where reality sets in for the apprentice as leaders give students an opportunity to help lead in a certain area. For example, if someone is being developed to lead in a small group, the person might lead a Q&A time. That would be followed with feedback from the leader.

3. You Do. I Help. Too often, this transitioning stage is where many churches fail. In Jesus's ministry, He sent the 12 disciples to heal the sick, raise the dead, cleanse lepers, and cast out demons (Matt. 10:5–15). This apprenticeship relationship transitions from supporting to helping the leader. This development stage is the system of training the new generation of practitioners with on-the-job training. The more experienced leader begins releasing responsibilities to the new developing leader.

4. You Do. I Watch. In the final stage, the disciples do the work and become the leaders. Jesus delegates responsibility and authority: "All authority in heaven and on earth has been given to me" (Matt. 28:18). The process of leadership development is almost complete as the new leader grows confident and competent in his or her role.

Jesus didn't take these men and immediately throw them into leadership. Instead, He walked with them, prayed with them, and discipled them. Making disciples as Jesus did takes hard work. It requires nurturing time, emotional intelligence, capacity, and fortitude. If you want a healthy church, you need to develop leaders. To prevent burnout among leaders, focus on discipling leaders so they can also lead.

The Five Stages of Discipleship

Churches are finding it difficult to create a solid, simple discipleship path to help regular attendees, as well as newcomers, take the next steps in their walk with Christ. Many churches have an overwhelming number of programs available but no cohesive path that helps people learn which steps to take and when. Based on Jesus's commission to His followers when He left Earth, this is a big problem.

Part of the problem with disciple-making is that people do not know where or how to assess where people are. Here are some ways to know where the people in your church are in the stages of discipleship. The following graph and list[8] will help you create a roadmap and apply scripture to the lives of your people.

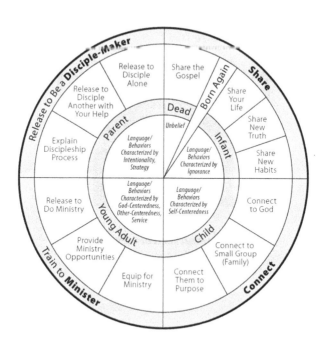

1. Spiritually dead (Eph. 2:1–5)
   - I don't believe there's a God.
   - The Bible is just a bunch of errors.
   - There are many ways a person can get to God.
   - I don't believe in hell.
   - I've been a good person, so when I die, everything will be okay.
2. Infant (1 Pet. 2:2–3)
   - Do I need to go to church regularly?
   - How can I pray and regularly read my Bible?
   - I don't need anyone else. It's just me and Jesus.
   - I need someone to regularly care for me.
   - I just got baptized, but I still have problems in my life. I thought Jesus was supposed to take care of all my problems.
3. Children (1 Cor. 3:2)
   - I can't wait to go to church to get fed.
   - No one ever says hi to me at church. I don't know if this church is meeting my needs anymore.
   - Don't split my small group into two. I won't get to be with my friends.
   - Who are all these new people coming to our church? The church is getting too big.
   - I didn't like the music today. Why do we have to learn new songs?
4. Young Adult (1 John 2:13–14)
   - In my devotions, I came across something I have a question about.
   - I really want to go to Senegal on a mission trip this summer.
   - I love serving in the church. I can see how God has gifted me and is using me.

- Someone is looking to join a group at our church. Is there a good group, or can we start a new one?
- Someone missed our small group, so I called them to see if they were doing alright.

5. Parent (2 Tim. 2:1–2)
   - I feel like God is calling me to invest in a few people at our church so they can mature in their faith.
   - I've been praying for my friend at work. He asked me to explain the Bible to him. Would you pray for me as I spend time in the word with him?
   - Our small group is going on a mission trip together. I am praying for God's wisdom as I give each person a different responsibility to help them grow.
   - The greatest task of discipleship for me is with my family and our children.
   - I want to be conscious of the influence of my words and actions around others.

Discipleship in Every Part of Ministry

I may sound like a broken record by now, but it should be obvious. Every church not only *should* but *must* embrace the mission of making disciples. I would even say that if you don't make disciples, you are living in sin. Every person called to salvation is called to discipleship. The church has been given one task: to go make disciples.

Many church leaders get excited about the idea of making disciples and zealously preach about it for a while, but whenever they run into a problem, the story changes. As soon as it gets too difficult and the price is too high, they drop the idea all together. In order to make discipleship happen, we not only need a vision but also a system to sustain the process. One thing we cannot leave out is intentional discipleship. In fact, not being involved in it is the biggest thing the church could neglect, for not only the church as a whole but for every Christian individual on their journey to maturity. It is not a metaphorical or spatial journey; we all are on a journey of discipleship. But how well are we doing?

> Every church not only *should* but *must* embrace the mission of making disciples. I would even say that if you don't make disciples, you are living in sin.

Unfortunately, we are not doing so well. I believe that is how we will be marked and evaluated as a church. A decision must be made daily to devote yourself to the call of making disciples.

What's amazing is how many people are not anywhere close to being mature. And if you don't have a grievance with yourself for not making disciples, then shame on you. If we don't do it, we have sinned and disappointed our God. Churches have become preoccupied with existing to meet people's needs and satisfy their wants. Churches are no longer fellowships of those who are sacrificial, who want to give their lives away.

It's time for a change. But change only happens when people's pain associated with the status quo is greater than the pain associated with change. True change happens for leaders when the pain of staying the same becomes greater than the pain of change.

Where Will We End Up?

Chapter 6

A Costly Commitment

When Christ calls a man, he bids him come and die.

—Dietrich Bonhoeffer

"If this gospel is such good news," asked a young man, "where have you all been? What have you been doing in the community? The church wasn't there when I needed you, and suddenly you want to be involved in my life. Well, I don't have time for that. How does what you say you believe relate to how Jesus lived?"

Sadly, this man was spot-on. Christians sadly are known more for their hate speech, arguments, stinginess, and ignorance. As I meet churches in general, I don't confront a lot of Christ-like people. I wonder what the thoughts of a lost person are when entering a church. Would unbelievers look to professing Christians and be drawn to Jesus? As Mahatma Gandhi, a Hindu believer, once said, "I like your Christ, I do not like your Christians. Your Christians are so unlike your Christ."[1]

Jesus's Warning for Believers

Jesus warns those who claim to be disciples but do not obey Him. "Not everyone who says to me, 'Lord, Lord,' will enter the kingdom of heaven. . . . And then will I declare to them, 'I never knew you; depart from me, you workers of lawlessness.'" (Matt. 7:21, 23). This clear teaching is often ignored, and it determines how many will be judged in eternity.

How can we truly know whether someone is truly saved? Some might say, "Well, I know I'm saved because my mom, my dad, my pastor, everybody else told me I was saved." What would they do at the judgment seat? Others might say, "Well, because I prayed a prayer when I was young at a kid's Bible camp." Is a person saved because they prayed a little prayer? Even others might say, "Well, I feel in my heart of hearts that I'm saved." Is that because they have believed? Let's pause for a moment and think about this.

How do we know who has believed? Is it because everybody says they have believed? Is it because they say, "Well, I think I'm saved." "There is a way that seems right to a man, but its end is the way to death" (Prov. 14:12). On the basis of God's eternal decree, only those who have been saved are in the continual process of being changed (discipleship), and their style of life is walking in the path of God's truth (sanctification).

I cannot look into the heart. Even if I did, I am often easily deceived by my own heart. But "the fountain of wisdom is a bubbling brook" (Prov. 18:4), and "as [a man] thinketh in his heart, so is he" (Prov. 23:7 KJV). You are what you love.[2] The fruit of your life is the root of your heart.[3]

The problem here is that being a disciple is characterized by the implicit clash between those who understand their faith from merely the four Gospels, topped off with a few bits of Pauline statements (e.g., the Romans Road to Salvation, Rom. 3:23, 5:8, 6:23, 10:9–10) based on a few passages with a few illustrations of the gospel.

> The fruit of your life is the root of your heart.

Jesus said, "Every healthy tree bears good fruit, but the diseased tree bears bad fruit. A healthy tree cannot bear bad fruit, nor can a diseased tree bear good fruit. Every tree that does not bear good fruit is cut down and thrown into the fire. Thus you will recognize them by their fruits" (Matt. 7:17–20).

Imagine for a moment that Jesus is teaching this passage, and we are sitting in the crowd listening. Then He looks at you and me and says, "Thistles, thistles. Do you find thistles on fig trees?" And you respond, "Of course not, Jesus. I mean, you're not an agriculturalist; you're not a farmer. I mean, you're a carpenter. But everybody knows, Jesus, you don't find thorns on fig trees."

"Well, then, let me ask you another question," adds Jesus. "Do you find figs—good fruit—on thorn trees?"

"Why, no, Jesus. That's absolutely ridiculous. I mean, you're never going to find thorns on a fig tree, and you're not going to find figs on a thorn tree, Jesus. To say that could be possible—if anyone tells you that, Jesus, you can mark it down that they're either crazy or they're a liar."

> This is the truth—the reality of the Gospel is that it's either 100 percent true or 100 percent false. The fact that it's 100 percent true should drastically change how we live.

And then Jesus responds to you, "Well then, those who call themselves my disciples and bear bad fruit—would that not be the same as saying they were either lying or out of their mind to make such a statement?"

"Well, Jonathan, I've always just been this way," you might say. If you have always been what you've always been, then you need to ask if you've ever really met Jesus. Based on Christ's statement, it is better to simply admit that people who live like non-Christians are most likely non-Christians. Meeting Jesus changes everything. This is the truth—the reality of the Gospel is that it's either 100 percent true or 100 percent false. The fact that it's 100 percent true should drastically change how we live.

Jesus's Standard of a Costly Discipleship

An indication of growth in Christ-likeness is bearing fruit. The transformed mind informs the will, and from the will, we act. Your belief impacts your behavior since your belief system fuels your behavioral pattern. The Christian's fear of being considered judgmental has caused some to toss the theology of the gospel out the window.

How is it that so many people today profess to have had an encounter with Jesus Christ, and yet they are not permanently changed? Let's go back to the question that we raised earlier— How will you know if someone is a genuine disciple? It is by their fruit (Matt. 7:16). Examine yourself to see if you are in the faith (2 Cor. 13:5). Work out your own salvation with fear and trembling (Phil. 2:12), not on the basis of other believers in your church but according to your walk in light of the scriptures (1 John 1:7). Take a little reality check about your talk (Eph. 4:29). Do you laugh about the very things that God abhors? (Prov. 6:16). What do you treasure most in your heart? (Matt. 6:21). Is Christ the center of it all? (1 Cor. 1:1–9). Or is He just another to-do list in your life? The scripture is true. You will always know them by their fruit.

This is a gospel problem at the heart of it all. This is too radical of a stance. It goes absolutely contrary to the historic stand we've had as Protestants for the past 500 years. The church is then left in a huge theological confusion that leads believers to avoid it in grave pathological frustration.

Cheap Grace

Bonhoeffer's definition of cheap grace is churches preaching a Christianity without the cost involved; hence, the adjective *cheap* to describe it.[4] They preach forgiveness but not repentance, baptism but not church discipline, communion but not confession. Cheap grace is grace without the cross, grace without Jesus Christ. As a result, churches are crowded with a whole lot of confused people. We have set the bar too low. We do not expect growth, and we certainly don't expect reproduction.

So why don't believers want to make disciples and see our churches grow? Here are a few reasons why churches are struck and paralyzed from being able to reach the community:

1. We'd rather have our hands clean; we don't want to get messy.

It's a sad reality. We don't want the drug addicts, the prostitutes, or the felons just out of prison in our churches. But if we want to look more like Jesus, we have to reconsider it. E. Stanley Jones said, "Three words were constantly upon Jesus' lips: the least, the last, and the lost."[5]

You have to get your hands dirty. Discipleship is down-and-dirty, ugly, and really messy. You find out people's dirt. We must not be afraid to be honest about the mess we call real life. That's something few people want to do.

For this reason, you may have a greater distance between the pastor and the congregation than ever before. Throughout history, pastors have lived incarnate lives among the community and lived in or near the church in a parsonage. We see pastors leaving the city where their urban churches are located and living in the suburbs, driving into the city to minister. The distance between the pastor and the congregation means there is less life-on-life engagement and moral accountability with each other. Sadly, pastors often do not have any relationships with their flock. As my mentor once told me, "You're not a pastor, Jonathan, unless you find wool on your shoulder." A pastor can't be a pastor without the sheep.

2. We want the easy way out; we excuse ourselves at the altar of busyness.

Relationships take time, but we don't want to take the time. In reality, too busy is a myth. People make time for the things that are really important to them. Busyness makes us stop caring about the things we ought to care about most, for time is a daily treasure that attracts many robbers. Busyness robs us of being able to do things that really matter on God's agenda. It's not about *having* time, it's about *making* time. Kevin DeYoung said in his book *Crazy Busy*, "Busyness does not mean you are a faithful or fruitful Christian. It only means you are busy just like everyone else."[6]

Yes, life is crazy busy for all of us. So stop using the excuse of being busy. I am busy, too. Change or die, for our excuses are choking the life out of the church, and we don't even notice it. Nobody is too busy. It's just a matter of priorities.

> Busyness makes us stop caring about the things we ought to care about most, for time is a daily treasure that attracts many robbers.

Churches grow when they have the priority of making disciples. We must first begin as the pastor leading the staff and the staff leading and building other leaders. Until the staff level gets it, the people in the pews won't.

3. We want to stay in the pulpit; we do not live among the people.

I think at times (most of the time), it is a lot easier when we are just in the spotlight preaching for 30 to 40 minutes, driving back home, and then doing the same thing the following week.

Why? Because then you really don't have to care about real-life issues. The pastor doesn't have to see the people or be held accountable. And the flock continues to do the same thing over and over again. Rather than doing life 24/7 as Jesus did with His disciples, the church has become where people attend on Sundays rather than people who gather as a family. Perhaps that is why Matthew Henry lamented some preachers in the pulpit, "preaching so well that it is a pity they should ever come out; but, when out of the pulpit, living so ill that it is a pity they should ever come in."[7]

4. We want to do church work; we don't want to do Christ work.

Christ wants us to love people in an authentic relationship, but Sunday morning for many is a showcase of our best selves. Most of us don't want to be real and let our guards down. We are, in a sense, like the Pharisees who said something like this: *Jesus, thank you that I'm not like that person over there* (Luke 18:9–14). As a follower of Jesus, you will be tempted to compare yourself to other disciples. That is rarely helpful and often causes great damage. Until we get past that, we are not going to make an impact for the kingdom ministry.

The Whole Bible for the Whole Christian

The church has exchanged the theology of Paul's epistles for a self-centered lie. The lie has become a detrimental endemic in twenty-first century evangelical theology. The gospel we've preached has had a self-defeating effect on churches. We must not shy away from the truth about what we believe and what we do. We have already seen how important it is for our actions to match our beliefs, or what we claim to be our beliefs. The difficulty in achieving it is that we often deceive ourselves. We shy away from the truth about what we believe and what we do. Our actions must match our belief system, or what we claim to be our belief system. If we are not able to achieve it, we deceive ourselves.

Believers are called to be the salt of the Earth (Matt. 5:13–16), giving the flavor of Christ's life and mission to the world (Col. 4:6).

83

If that's not how Christians are characterized— by taste to the lost, dying, and perishing—the world will never catch the flavor (Mark 9:50).

In Luke 14:25–35, Jesus speaks of the cost of discipleship when He tells the multitude that whoever doesn't hate his mother or father is not worthy of being a disciple. We are comfortable with a discipleship that does not call us to total allegiance to Christ. In that passage, Jesus says to the crowds that no one can be His disciple unless he or she first hates his family (Luke 14:26). And the one who cannot bear his own cross cannot be His disciple (Luke 14:27). What does that mean when it is applied to the dedication of disciples? Jesus said something like this: *Sit down and count the cost of discipleship. You must leave home and family and travel on mission for me. You must depend on those you meet and witness to for your food and necessities.* Every material possession is left behind, with no thought of ever returning to reclaim it. We are not dedicated to possessions. Dedication to Christ is dedication to life without material resources to fall back on.

All followers of Christ are called to be the salt of the Earth, giving the flavor of Christ's life and mission to the world. If that's not how Christians are characterized, then the lost, dying, and perishing world will never taste the flavor. Being salty like Christ is a prerequisite for the journey. The bottom line is that this is an absolute oxymoron since salt can never lose its saltiness. Jesus is making a blatantly absurd statement because if you are in Christ, you will be salty since He is the salt. If people who are born-again disciples say they are not salty, it is an absurd, ridiculous statement. Christ says that those who call themselves disciples yet do not have flavor are not even fit for the manure pile. Their religion, as James says, is useless rubbish. In other words, such a life is a piece of trash.

As a follower of Christ, there are parts of the Bible I personally dislike and want to remove altogether. "If anyone would come after me, let him deny himself and take up his cross daily and follow me" (Luke 9:23). It is hard to follow after Jesus, but a radical approach to reading difficult passages can help you understand their plain meaning.

A. W. Tozer said, "And we must not select a few favorite passages to the exclusion of others. Nothing less than a whole Bible can make a whole Christian."[8] Basing all understanding of discipleship solely on the Romans Road could be missing the point. This shift from gospel culture to salvation culture has weakened the church and diminished the lives of Christians.

Excuses, Excuses, Excuses

Everyone agrees—discipleship is important and fundamental to the church and every facet of it. But since discipleship requires relationships that require time, the reality is that people don't want to take the time. They don't want the cost of it. You can make an excuse, or you can make a difference—but you can't do both.

Let's let Bonhoeffer sum it up for us with his most enduring source of wisdom on the demands of Christian discipleship:

Costly grace is the gospel which must be *sought* again and again and again, the gift which must be *asked* for, the door at which a man must *knock*. Such grace is *costly* because it calls us to follow, and it is *grace* because it calls us to follow *Jesus Christ*. It is costly because it costs a man his life, and it is grace because it gives a man the only true life. It is costly because it condemns sin, and grace because it justifies the sinner. Above all, it is *costly* because it cost God the life of his Son: "ye were bought at a price," and what has cost God much cannot be cheap for us. Above all, it is *grace* because God did not reckon his Son too dear a price to pay for our life, but delivered him up for us. Costly grace is the Incarnation of God.[9]

> You can make an excuse, or you can make a difference—but you can't do both.

I pray that all of us will change for the sake of the display of the beauty and the glory of God. May we refocus our faith and inspire discipleship lived out in a costly manner as we consider the words that Bonhoeffer lived out. It's time for us to stop making excuses and start making disciples, because this is not an optional command. Discipleship is not complete until the mentee becomes the mentor, or the disciple becomes the disciple-maker.

Simple, but Not Easy

Discipleship is simple, but it isn't easy. It's like losing weight. To lose weight, you have to do two things: eat healthy and exercise. Success so often lies within persistence. It's simple, but it's not easy.

In the midst of the hurricane of anxiety, may you look to Christ, the captain of the ship of your heart. In the midst of the cold hand of doubt that reminds you of your past identity, may you turn to Jesus the redeemer who is the anchor of your soul.[10] As a result, Jesus, the light of the world, will calm and clear the raging sea of your life so you can continue walking on the path of discipleship of ordinary radicals. The command to witness is given to all followers of Christ (Acts 1:8). Jesus commanded the apostles to preach the gospel to all creation. Jesus promised them, "I am with you always, to the end of the age" (Matt. 28:20).

The question for us, then, is this: What are we doing in order to, like Paul, risk all things (Phil. 3:8–10), even imprisonment (Acts 16:16–40)? Are we willing to see the kingdom of God advance throughout our community, and what is our role in advancing the gospel of Christ (Matt. 6:10)? Let's not just take this truth and bypass it (James 1:23). Let's remember that we are called to fulfill the Great Commission at whatever cost.

Chapter 7

A Call for All

If I have a pulse I have purpose.

—Kathie Lee Gifford

I didn't grow up in a typical Christian home. I was born in a family with a mother who was a devout believer and a father who was a dogmatic atheist. My father had a major anger problem and physically abused my mother. I was in great fear of him. In spite of the situation, many nights I got on my knees beside my bed and prayed, "Jesus, please save my dad." But things simply escalated and got worst, and I began to doubt God and eventually walked away from Him.

At age 12, I began spending time with gang members and became addicted to the behavioral pattern of this sinful world. I was a very angry, depressed young man. By the age of 15, I decided to run away from home. I was a morally corrupt, sin-loving God-hater. Then, in September, I was picked up by the police. I got kicked out of school, left the gang, and left the girl I was with. It was then that I began to seek the Lord. I had no hope but Jesus.

I heard the gospel at age 16. A pastor shared and said, "Jonathan, Jesus loved me, saved me, and changed me, and that is more than enough." For the very first time in my life, I decided to profess Jesus Christ as lord, to the glory of the father. I met Jesus, and my life has never been the same. Everything changed when Christ came into my life.

I don't think I knew what it meant at the moment, but I began my journey to grow as a disciple of Christ. After I was saved, God opened up the opportunity for me to go back to high school. I began to read the Bible and pray. I was involved with a youth group, church gatherings, Bible study, and prayer meeting. Then it dawned on me—Jesus delivered the Great Commission. With it came the command for all people on Earth to be reached with the good news.

> God isn't interested in simply tweaking our behavior or stepping up our morality. He is all about radically transforming our entire life.

But who was Jesus speaking to? Was it to the original apostles only? To the church at large? To certain local churches? Or was it given to each and every Christian? Is discipleship a choice for the Christian or a necessary part of being a Christian? If so, then what am I doing with my life? I don't want to waste this life that has been entrusted to me.

I believe the call to discipleship is a fundamental redirection of our human existence. God isn't interested in simply tweaking our behavior or stepping up our morality. He is all about radically transforming our entire life.[1] It is a reorientation, an all-embracing turnabout of our lives so our affections might be placed primarily on Christ.

In order to grow bigger, you must structure bigger with a bigger vision. Here are a few core doctrinal issues that hinder churches in the task of discipleship:

1. Scriptural authority and Sufficiency: Power (Heb. 4:12)

In American churches, the task of a pastor is a biblically glorified CEO of a corporation with some sort of mission statement.

You don't find that in the Bible. Instead, Paul cast a vision that calls upon every shepherd and teacher "to equip the saints for the work of ministry, for building up the body of Christ" (Eph. 4:12 RSV). Those 16 words are the pastor's mission statement from God.

John Piper said, "We pastors are being killed by the professionalizing of the pastoral ministry. The mentality of the professional is not the mentality of the prophet. It is not the mentality of the slave of Christ. Professionalism has nothing to do with the essence and heart of the Christian ministry. The more professional we long to be, the more spiritual death we will leave in our wake."[2]

The mentality of professionalism has crippled and weakened the effectiveness of the local church body. The more professional we long to be, the more spiritual death we will bring upon ourselves. There is no such thing as a professional childlike faith (Matt. 18:3), nor is there a professional tender kindness (Eph. 4:32).

We need more competent disciple-makers who are trained in biblical soul care from the ground level, applying the gospel of grace and truth to the multifaceted brokenness in people's lives.

2. Progressive sanctification: Hope (Rom. 15:4)

Progressive sanctification—that is perhaps one of the biggest problems in our current seminary programs. Most master of divinity programs focus on the clergy serving in a pulpit ministry, preaching the word (the public ministry of the word). There is even a culture in seminaries of exalting a preaching ministry as a glorious task. As a result, many young seminarians rarely hear about the shepherding side of the day-to-day tasks with the flock through discipleship (the private ministry of the word).

I sensed this in my first pastorate in Chicago in an inner-city ministry setting when the daunting question was set before me in my office: How can I possibly help all the people whose lives are overflowing with troubles, conflicts, and emotional problems of every kind?

The church is a place of real-life change. In order to see that, we not only must disciple, but disciple well. The problem within the church is that people are not discipled, so they don't know what to do and consequently don't do anything. Church leadership with this view of the gospel has led to the belief that disciples are just made automatically in the Christian process (progressive sanctification). Disciples are not made by accident or automatically; there must be an intentional plan in place in order for them to be made consistently.

We need a model that doesn't simply end on a theory level but one that is a single thought-shaping, heart-engaging, ministry-guiding, word-selecting commitment for the sake of the gospel.

3. Priesthood of all believers and community: Love (John 13:35)

The local church is caught in a consumer-mentality gospel. That means reaching and teaching must go beyond the twenty-first century mentality of checking into a church and then mentally checking out. Bill Hull recognizes this problem when he writes, "The evangelical church has become weak, flabby, and too dependent on artificial means that can only simulate real spiritual power. Churches are too little like training centers to shape up the saints.... The average Christian resides in the comfort zone of 'I pay the pastor to preach, administrate, and counsel.... I am the consumer, he is the retailer.... I have the needs, he meets them....That's what I pay for.'"[3]

Pastors have been trained to act as caregivers rather than transformers. The average pastor spends 95 percent of the time taking care of members rather than transforming and leading them to be like Jesus.[4]

A pastor is called not only to do ministry but to help others learn how to do it. That model that Paul set forth flies in the face of this consumer-mentality Christianity. Therefore, discipleship is not simply staffed by elite, paid clergy. Instead, it is God's call for all the saints (the priesthood of believers) to biblically counsel and disciple all.

The average church on Sunday morning is far too much like a college football game on Saturday afternoon—66,000 people badly in need of exercise watching 22 young men badly in need of rest.[5]

We Need to Say No to Some Good Things

Every Christian should be helping other believers become more mature in Christ. Every church should think through how biblical disciple-making can be expressed in corporate life. Our current methods are getting the current results. Robby Gallaty, in his book *Growing Up*, puts it this way:

> When the church becomes an end in itself, it ends. When Sunday school, as great as it is, becomes an end in itself, it ends. When small groups ministry becomes an end in itself, it ends. When the worship service becomes an end in itself, it ends. What we need is for discipleship to become the goal, and then the process never ends. The process is fluid. It is moving. It is active. It is a living thing. It must continue to go on. Every disciple must make disciples.[6]

Here are three church practices that need to die in order for the church to return to Christ-centered discipleship:

1. No more binge-watching

The church is filled with people who think they are participating in the mission while binge-watching from the sidelines and criticizing how others are making disciples. To be a disciple of Jesus is to participate in God's redemptive mission for the world. As we read scripture, we notice that Jesus's disciples rarely engage His mission as individuals (Matt. 10:5–15; Luke 9:1–27, 10:1–24).

As a disciple of Jesus, you are part of the church (Rom. 12:4–5, 1 Cor. 12:12–17, Col. 1:18). The goal of a church must be to present every Christian to God "mature in Christ" (Col. 1:28). The church is called by Jesus to "make disciples of all nations" (Matt. 28:19). This evangelistic work of declaring the gospel is the primary ministry the church has in the world.

The church and the kingdom of God are not one and the same.

1. The church is not the kingdom (Acts 8:12, 19:8, 20:25, 28:23, 31).
2. The kingdom creates the church (Matt. 21:43).
3. The church witnesses to the kingdom (Matt. 24:14).
4. The church is the instrument of the kingdom (Matt. 10:8, Luke 10:17).
5. The church is the custodian of the kingdom (Matt. 16:19).

Eventually Jesus will return, and his kingdom reign will extend over all creation (1 Cor. 15:24–28). Therefore, you have inherited the continued mission to spread the gospel message to the end of the Earth. That doesn't mean you're obligated to become a missionary, but it does mean you have been called to play a part in proclaiming the gospel throughout all nations.[7] The church should fulfill the overarching banner of the vision to make disciples.

The gospel establishes peace for us both vertically and horizontally—with God and with our neighbor. With Jesus's ascension, you've inherited His commission and His command to serve as His witness "in Jerusalem and in all Judea and Samaria, and to the end of the earth" (Acts 1:8). The gospel includes three relationships:

1. Intrapersonal (relationship with God)
2. Interpersonal (home and work)
3. Extrapersonal (society and community)

Obviously, you can't fulfill any of those charges by yourself. You need to be part of something bigger, something capable of reaching your community and outward to the entire world.[8] The good news is that the Great Commission is so wonderfully freeing because it is big enough to fill the whole world and yet small enough for every single one of us to play a part.

God's will for your life is that you come to know Jesus in a deeper, more personal way, grow in your relationship with Him, and use your gifts to advance His mission for the world through the community of the church.[9]

2. No more Pulpit-hoarding

"Now when they saw the boldness of Peter and John, and perceived that they were uneducated, common men, they were astonished. And they recognized that they had been with Jesus" (Acts 4:13). As believers, sometimes we forget that God wants to use unschooled ordinary people to change the world.

Dwight L. Moody, one of the greatest evangelists of the nineteenth century, said, "If this world is going to be reached, I am convinced that it must be done by men and women of average talent."[10] He was an extremely average man without much talent or potential. His education ended in the fifth grade, he couldn't spell, and his grammar was awful. But he left a great mark on history. This unordained shoe salesman, whose manners were often brash and crude, was a man who felt God's call to preach the gospel. Who would have thought someone like Moody would become one of the greatest evangelists the world has ever known?

He was saved in 1856 at the age of 18, and by the end of his life, he had spoken about the gospel to more than 100 million people throughout the world. On several occasions, he filled stadiums with capacities of 2,000 to 4,000 people. Famous preacher Charles Spurgeon invited him to speak and promoted him as well. When

Moody returned to the United States, crowds of 12,000 to 20,000 were as common as they had been in England.

Moody's vision was to train men and women in the work of reaching other people. Moody believed that we must train people to stand in the gap between the laity and the ministers. What if everyone in your church saw their primary vocation as a harvest and kingdom worker? As Moody said, "No one can sum up all God is able to accomplish through one solitary life, wholly yielded, adjusted, and obedient to Him."[11]

A recent study by Barna Group came up with some interesting statistics. Its president, David Kinnaman, said, "There are now more full-time senior pastors who are over the age of 65 than under the age of 40."[12] As the average pastor grows older in America, churches say they are struggling to find young Christians who want to become future pastors. That is a discipleship problem.

We have Millennials leaving the church and fewer young pastors. There is a real need for young pastors to fill the gap between the generations. The Millennial generation craves pastors who understand their desire for relationships and experiencing God.[13] Young pastors from that generation could bridge the gap. Older pastors, it's time to let the next generation take over. Disciple them, mentor them, equip them, and train them intentionally through a relational environment.

3. No more passive mentality

In the early church, it was an exciting and confusing time for the earliest disciples of Jesus (Col. 3:11, Eph. 2:14–16). They were exciting times because of the many ways in which God's Spirit moved to accomplish mighty things (Acts 2:41–47). They were sometimes confusing because the earliest disciples were still figuring out what it meant to live as followers of Christ in their everyday lives (2 Tim. 4:3–4, 1 Pet. 1:12–21, 2 Pet. 3:14–18, 1 John 4:1–6).

That's why the epistles are so important. These letters clarify important elements of the Christian life, including the importance of discipleship. The church has an obligation to nurture those who are already believers and build them up to maturity in the faith (Col. 1:28, Eph. 4:12–13). The goal of a church must be to present every Christian "mature in Christ" (Col. 1:28). Living as a disciple of Jesus includes embracing a lifestyle of discipleship. Therefore, by definition, a follower of Christ is called to grow toward maturity in Jesus and help others do the same. Discipleship is that simple—nothing more, nothing less. There is no such thing as a passive, purposeless lifestyle of those who embrace Jesus but do not obey the will of Christ.

What Is the Silver Bullet?

What if the silver bullet to kicking off a new season of growth didn't start with some kind of new model? What if we have simply been ignoring the basic model that Christ has already laid before us as a church? As Daniel Im said, "I am convinced that ignorance is the main reason churches in North America, and in many parts of the world, are not experiencing growth."[14]

Calling yourself a disciple but not a disciple-maker is missing the whole point. A disciple makes disciples. If you're a fisherman but you don't smell like fish, you're not a fisherman. We are not disciples by proxy.

Discipleship is a community project, not just a personal pursuit (Heb. 10:24–25). Every Christian should be helping other believers become more mature in Christ (1 Cor. 14:20). The church has an obligation to nurture those who are already believers and build them up to maturity in the faith (Col. 1:28,

> Calling yourself a disciple but not a disciple-maker is missing the whole point. A disciple makes disciples.

Eph. 4:12–13). It is clearly contrary to the New Testament pattern to think that our only goal is to bring people to initial saving faith. We should help others grow in Christ. Within the fellowship of the church, there are certain means of grace—activities, ceremonies, and functions. Grace within the fellowship of the church inspires more grace in the community.

The community must be the local church because Jesus has given it unique authority to preach the gospel, baptize believers into faith and church membership, and teach obedience to Christ. Every church should think through how biblical disciples find expression in their corporate lives. Throughout history, God has done extraordinary things through ordinary people.

We Take Ourselves Way Too Seriously

Many pastors criticize me for taking the gospel so seriously. But do they really think that on judgment day, Christ will chastise me and say, "Jonathan, you took me way too seriously"?

> Many pastors criticize me for taking the gospel so seriously. But do they really think that on judgment day, Christ will chastise me and say, "Jonathan, you took me way too seriously"?

I think people often forget the simple gospel. Two thousand years ago, in the Middle East, an event occurred that permanently changed the world. Because of that event, history changed. Jesus rose from the dead (Matt. 28:5–6, John 20:27–29). Nobody else has ever done that. And Jesus's resurrection has changed history and the world (1 Cor. 15:14). It has changed me and millions of others. That changes the way we live life here on Earth (2 Cor. 5:17).

Jesus didn't just come to make bad people good. He came to make dead people alive (Mark 2:17). He is coming back

(Matt. 25:13). We get to teach this every day, encouraging one another (Heb. 10:24–25, Matt. 24:44) and making the Great Commission our great priority.

Chapter 8

Multiplication for Exponential Growth

If your ministry has a leadership problem
it has a discipleship problem. You can't make
disciples and not develop leaders.

—Bill Hull

I love history. I love it because it teaches us so much about our current state and how to move forward. Let's take a quick look at the explosion of the early church.

At the time of Jesus's crucifixion, there were 120 believers (Acts 1:14–15). The book of Acts is a record of how Acts 1:8 became reality in the first 40 years of the church's existence. At the close of Acts, disciples had been made and churches established from Jerusalem to Judea and Samaria (Acts 1:8) and then throughout Asia Minor into Macedonia, Greece, and across the Adrian Sea even to Rome. Sociologist Rodney Starks said the number of Christians grew to about six million by AD 300 (before Constantine).[1] The first 12 disciples, empowered by the Holy Spirit and commissioned by Jesus, transformed the whole world. The question for us is this: Why doesn't that seem to match up with our current state of the church?

In just 300 years, Christianity grew from a small Jewish sect in Galilee to the dominant religion of the Roman Empire. I don't know about you, but six million Christians seems like an impossible number. However, when we look at the multiplication equation, you only need a growth rate of about 40 percent per decade to get there.

That is an annual growth of 4 percent. That's it! That seems a very doable number to me. The early growth of the Christian church is impressive, but not so impressive that it's not doable.

Stagnant, Lifeless, Dead Churches

Unfortunately, many churches don't reach the point of multiplication. Churches are notorious for being stagnant. Daniel Im said, "Churches that multiply understand, that multiplication begins with discipleship."[2] The Great Commission is crucial not only for the commitment to grow but to multiply as well. But how does a church grow without development and discipleship? Today, people are an audience rather than an army (Eph. 4:12). Because God has called Christians to be soldiers, the role of a pastor is to equip the people for the work of the ministry (2 Tim 3:16–17, Heb. 13:20–21).

> A church that multiplies is unstoppable. The sad truth is that most churches are not functioning this way. We are on a model of addition rather than multiplication.

If we are not making disciples, why are we here? If only our churches lived out discipleship, we would be so much more effective in reaching our community. When a church fosters a culture of Christian discipleship and growth (2 Tim. 2:2), it multiplies believers' efforts for missions domestically and internationally. A church that multiplies is unstoppable. The sad truth is that most churches are not functioning this way. We are on a model of addition rather than multiplication.

Push-Back on a Biblical Model of Multiplication

So, our church hires pastors to not do ministry? Let me get this straight. We are going to pay pastors to train us to do their jobs? Yes, because it is biblical. We are all ministers, and we have a role to play in the kingdom. Look at the graphic below from *Designed to Lead* by Eric Geiger and Kevin Peck.[3]

The Typical Approach
Pastors ⟶ Minister ⟶ People[4]

The system makes sense, really. People come to church and generously give money. So as the church grows, more money can be given to compensate ministers. But if the church is not careful, it can subtly be taught that it is paying people to do ministry. We are to prepare, not perform.

The Biblical Model
Pastors ⟶ Prepare ⟶ People ⟶ Minister ⟶ Each Other[5]

Unlike the typical model that fosters and develops consumers and moochers, the biblical model develops more participants and contributors. The ministry is for all who are called to share in Christ's life, but the pastorate is for those who possess the peculiar gift of being able to help other men and women practice any ministry to which they are called.

Yes, it is easier and more comfortable to rely on pastors to do the ministry. And it takes time to build people, especially if that has not been the culture and practice of the church. Change is hard. People prefer what they have observed and known. As the old saying goes, better caught than taught. So in many churches, the cycle continues.

Another reason from a leadership standpoint is that leaders resist a culture change of equipping because of their own selfishness and insecurity. As John Maxwell said, "When leaders fail to empower others, it usually due to three main reasons:

1. Desire for job security
2. Resistance to change
3. Lack of self-worth"[6]

Yes, it is easier said than done. We all know that already. But part of our calling as leaders is not to simply call people to do, or worse, to do it all ourselves. Instead, we need to inspire, equip, and empower people. That means we need to do the foundational work of sharing the authority and responsibility of the vision and mission, not just delegating tasks.

"In today's church, leadership has become something of an obsession," said Albert Mohler.[7] There is a sense of lostness in the definition of leadership. The term *leadership* has been thrown around left to right and has ended up on the pedestal of worship. The obsession of extreme leadership has veered the church off-track. Leadership is a potent relationship between leader and follower. A leader is one who has followers. There is no escaping that simple fact. No followers mean no leader.

Leadership is what one does to get followers. I wish I'd known that before entering ministry. An old Chinese proverb says, "He who thinketh he leadeth and no one is following, is just talking a walk!"[8] Leadership is earned; therefore, leaders must earn a following by leading. A person can be in a leadership position in a church and not actually be a leader.

So leadership and discipleship are actually two sides of the same coin. Many pastors don't recognize that, but if you have a discipleship problem, you have a leadership problem.[9] Leadership is training leaders. Leaders don't create followers. They create more leaders to build up the kind of leaders who will champion the faith well into the future. Peter Drucker said that we must "keep the main thing the main thing."[10] If leadership is simply training leaders, then we must accurately assess individuals and systematically train them. Discipleship is intentionally equipping leaders through accountable relationships empowered by the spirit of God.

> Leadership and discipleship are actually two sides of the same coin. Many pastors don't recognize that, but if you have a discipleship problem, you have a leadership problem.

A culture of discipleship multiplies the gifts and ministries of the entire church body, not just the pastor or a few select leaders. By this method, we witness a cycle of reproduction to the ends of the earth to the end of time.[11] If you don't have a clear understanding of the gospel, chances are you are in a maintenance mode rather than a multiplication mode.

The Current State of the Church

The churches in North America tend to have people pray the prayer of salvation and then move on to someone else. The task of evangelism and discipleship is now given to the super Christian leadership (the addition model). The traditional church mentality is I will *do* the job rather than I will *develop* people to do the job. As Christians, we do well with Ephesians 2:8–9, but then we fall short. We never make it to Ephesians 4, developing leaders who then lead and nurture others to accomplish the Great Commission. We must look at the Great Commission with biblical conviction, step out in faith, and simply do it.

We must be careful to teach the right kind of discipleship. When we teach a form of discipleship that does not result in reproduction, we miss the mark. Without the succession plan for leadership, we start hiring people for the job rather than training them for leadership. We are not able to introduce each other to spiritual children and grandchildren if we don't have that in our mindset (2 Tim. 2:2). Training is what Jesus did with His disciples for three years. It is also what the early church did and what the apostle Paul did—person by person, city by city.

How the Early Church Grew

Addition Model – Winning 365,000 People per Year for 25 years.

Numbers	People	Numbers	People	Numbers	People
1	365,000	11	4,015,000	21	7,665,000
2	730,000	12	4,380,000	22	8,030,000
3	1,095,000	13	4,745,000	23	8,395,000
4	1,460,000	14	5,110,000	24	8,760,000
5	1,825,000	15	5,475,000	25	9,125,000
6	2,190,000	16	5,840,000		
7	2,555,000	17	6,205,000		
8	2,920,000	18	6,570,000		
9	3,285,000	19	6,935,000		
10	3,740,000	20	7,300,000		

Multiplication Model – One gifted pastor equipping 30 people so each one will win one person per year, doubling each year for 25 years.

Numbers	People	Numbers	People	Numbers	People
1	30	11	30,720	21	31,457,280
2	60	12	61,440	22	62,914,560
3	120	13	122,880	23	125,829,120
4	240	14	245,760	24	251,658,480
5	480	15	491,520	25	503,316,480
6	960	16	983,040		
7	1,920	17	1,966,080		
8	3,840	18	3,932,160		
9	7,680	19	7,864,320		
10	15,360	20	15,380,640		

Discipleship is based on multiplication, not addition. This plan was laid out by Jesus, and it has limitless potential for the sake of the gospel. It's hard because it takes more intentionality, time, thought, and effort. Pastors too often want to settle down with preaching to make disciples, but when we look at the life of Christ, we see that He invested in the few. Throughout the gospel accounts, we see Jesus spending time with the masses 17 times and 49 times with the few.

Multiplication forces you into leadership development. Here are some responses and excuses we often hear: "We don't know how. We don't have the expertise. We don't have the time. We don't have the framework and resources to make it happen." The framework many of us have learned is the conveyor-belt model, which puts training on cruise control without any destination.

"Well, Jonathan, I love doing rather than developing." I have heard that more than once. And the reason for that is that no one has developed you. There is this same excuse for discipleship: "Well, nobody discipled me, so I don't know how to do it. I was just thrown in and had to figure it out." Whether it is insecurity or conviction, the heart of the matter is that we are not giving the ministry away to our people.

How Can We Know If We Are Developing?

To answer this, we must ask the right question: Did we build these people, or did we buy these people? If we have bought most of the staff, then we have an issue. Sometimes, it's necessary to hire staff to start the discipleship process. However, if the church is healthy, it should be reproducing from within so the people will thrive in that context. (Note: Taking a healthy church audit may bring conviction.)

Three Forms of Leadership Development

1. Dumping = *telling and commanding*

Dumping is an old-school style of commanding people and telling them to do the task. They don't care about the people but just want to check them off their list. When Jesus said to go and make disciples, I don't think He meant send them to school. It seems like the best way to make disciples is like the bygone days of apprenticeship—very relational, hands-on, and life-invested.

2. Delegating = *teaching and training*

Delegating is a knowledge transfer through a traditional form of education. As you can already tell, that's a good attempt, but you haven't reached the goal. Dumping information doesn't produce transformation. An effective disciple-maker knows how to take discipleship from theory to practice, from the classroom to the living room.

3. Developing = modeling and coaching

Developing is when mentors are watching, interacting, and showing church leadership how to be servant leaders. This type of leadership development knows how someone got to where they are in their leadership and spiritual growth. This functions best in a relational environment. These leaders invest time in others, not as a project but as people.

In this process, they discover what discipleship and leadership are all about—development, not a transaction. Knowledge transfer is a transaction; however, development and discipleship are an overlap of knowledge, experience, and coaching.

The Need for Leadership Development

In seminary, students take a lot of homiletic (biblical exposition) classes on how to deliver sermons. But there are not many classes on leadership. You may be a solid communicator, but if you can't lead well, you'll severely cripple your congregation. In the last decade of church ministry, more and more leaders have stated the need for leadership classes in seminary. Every church needs leaders. Good leaders don't just magically show up at the front door of our churches.

In fact, recently in my church, someone was dumped into a position without clear expectation and guidance. That couldn't be more frustrating, not only for the leadership team but also for the lay congregants who were trying to follow. They knew something was a bit off, although they did not know why. Present helplessness can lead to future hopelessness, which causes churchgoers to jump to another church and continue doing the same thing over and over again, expecting a different result.

We must be thinking critically through the process of kingdom ministry. The process of recruiting and equipping is probably more important than we actually think. Too often, our leaders are desperate

> Too often, our leaders are desperate for recruitment. We must move from desperation to inspiration.

for recruitment. We must move from desperation to inspiration. We need a change of mindset. Recruiting is more than gathering warm bodies to make the system work. Recruiting is training up leaders who will train up more leaders.

1. Why build leaders? Because it is biblical.

Scripture give us a clear layout to follow. I couldn't help but recognize the similarity to Paul's description of the task of church leaders—"to equip the saints for the work of ministry, for building up the body of Christ" (Eph. 4:12). Leadership is building and equipping and preparing others to do the ministry to accomplish the church's objective. A biblical model of church leadership is necessary in order for the church to display the glory to the nations.

Methods will always vary. We see examples in scripture:

- Matthew 28:20 – Missionaries must teach the nations all that Jesus commanded.
- Acts 20:24 – Finish the course of ministry.
- Ephesians 6:4 – Fathers must train their children.
- 2 Timothy 2:2 – Paul trained young Timothy, and he trained others to train others.
- Titus 2:4 – Older women train younger women.
- 1 Peter 4:10 – All Christians use their gifts to train others.
- Hebrews 3:13 – All Christians are to exhort and stir one another up.

The ultimate goal of discipleship does not end with training leaders but leads to multiplying faithful followers of Christ.

2. Leadership that doesn't stay the same.

I am constantly reminded that my church is not about me. Christ is the head, and I am not (Eph. 4:15). But somehow, we think leadership will stay the same.

If the leadership team never changes or is always changing, both are warning signs. On the one hand, churches become ingrown when there is never any new blood among the leaders. If your elder board, leadership team, or Sunday school teachers are the same now as they were for the past decades or so, you have a problem. This is an indication that there is no multiplication or reproduction from within, and the church is cruising through a maintenance mode. The reason may be that the leaders fear job security or that they are lazy and don't disciple others. Or it may be that the church is not reaching out to the community.

Therefore, nothing is happening, and stagnation occurs. Jim Collins was correct in his book *Good to Great*. Stagnant organizations that want to grow must be willing to face the brutal facts.[12] The members of a local church should cultivate a culture of discipleship because they want to care for the next generation. Our job is to pass the baton to the next generation and let them run the race well (Heb. 12:1–3).

3. Vision so large that it vacuums in new leaders.

Paul instructed young Timothy, "And what you have heard from me in the presence of many witnesses entrust to faithful men, who will be able to teach others also" (2 Tim 2:2). Paul prays to deploy these devoted, faithful, future followers of Jesus to the nations. This task of the local church is critical to the mission of Christ.

It doesn't matter whether it's a megachurch or a small rural church. There are some large churches that have no plan to train leaders. They would rather bring in people from the outside than train them from the inside. If we hoard certain people to keep the show going, we prevent our next generations from growing into vacant positions. Mike Stachura said, "The mark of a great church is not its seating capacity, but its sending capacity!"[13] Releasing other leaders to lead doesn't make you less valuable; it makes you more valuable.

There are young men and women who are eager, able, and willing, but there is no vacancy for them to step into and rise up. Why are we losing all these people? Because people are going through the vacuum of the world, sucked up into obscurity.

Leadership Pipeline with a Discipleship Path

Does your church have an intentional development plan to disciple and deploy believers to live out the Great Commission? Does that happen haphazardly? When someone comes to your church, would they see evidence of the Great Commission in the congregants' lives?

Of course, Jesus was the greatest at developing leaders. His life was characterized by discipleship. He constantly poured his life and soul into a handful of disciples. He taught them to be disciple-makers and trusted that future generations would hear the good news because of their witness.

We Christians (disciples) have been given the joy and privilege of leadership development and equipping the saints. Your success as a disciple of Christ is not something you do; it is someone you disciple to also become a disciple-maker. Effective ministry is not gauged by how many ministries we execute but how well we equip others to partake in ministry.

> Your success as a disciple of Christ is not something you do; it is someone you disciple to also become a disciple-maker.

The ultimate goal of discipleship does not end with training leaders but with training leaders who are multiplying faithful followers of Christ. True success in our lives as disciples is growing those we are discipling. We are part of God's great plan, which spans from generation to generation. Let us not grow weary of doing good (Gal. 6:9). Be vigilant to train, equip, and build leaders for the sake of God's glory. Through God's grace and our guidance, they may witness God do more than we could ever imagine.

Our greatest fear should not be failure. It should be succeeding at things in life that don't really matter. The greatest challenge in discipleship is never a lack of talented leaders or money. It is us. It is often our selfish desire to control and our own unwillingness to release that prevent multiplication. Some leaders may need a little heart check.

What are you doing today to fulfill Acts 1:8?

1. Jerusalem (interpersonal level – family)
2. Judea (organizational level – business)
3. Samaria (societal level – community)

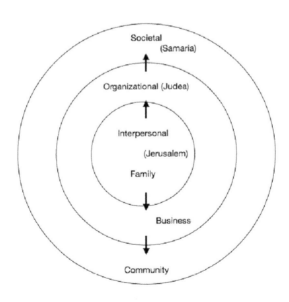

Conclusion

Start Small

When we say of a biblical command, "I don't think
that will work," what we have done is elevate
our reason above God's Word.

—Jonathan Hayashi

In this fallen world—even in this very complex, post-modern world—people are desperately hungry to hear the gospel of the Lord Jesus Christ. "The typical churched believer will die without leading a single person to a life-saving relationship with Jesus Christ," said Jim Putman from Real Life Ministries.[1]

Yes, there are many willing Christians who have absolutely no plan for discipleship because it is work for them. But before we go there, we must acknowledge that Christians don't practice discipleship because they have no idea how. Even church pastors have no idea what they are doing many times.

We are not speaking of becoming kinder and nicer, although those values matter greatly. We need a radical, revolutionary reshaping of what it means to make disciples and follow Jesus. Church leaders need to inspire, equip, and empower people.

Depend on the Holy Spirit

God works in various ways to bring people to salvation in Jesus Christ. It all begins when God calls us by His Holy Spirit. It is only by the Holy Spirit who calls a person by awakening his or her heart, mind, and soul to the personal need of salvation.

As the Westminster Confession says, "This effectual call is of God's free and special grace alone, not from anything at all foreseen in man, who is altogether passive therein, until, being quickened and renewed by the Holy Spirit, he is thereby enabled to answer this call, and to embrace the grace offered and conveyed in it."[2] It is only then that a person can truly accept and respond to the grace of God through faith.

Martin Luther said, "I believe that by my own reason or strength I cannot believe in Jesus Christ, my Lord, or come to him. But the Holy Spirit has called me through the Gospel, enlightened me with his gifts, and sanctified and preserved me in true faith."[3]

Don't Announce the Revolution

Change is extremely difficult, especially in an established church. When momentum is strong and energy is high, the last thing most churches are thinking about is changing a culture. Therefore, do not announce the revolution publicly. Begin to converse with the people in your circle. The conversation can change the culture and bring awareness to the issues.

> Change is extremely difficult, especially in an established church. When momentum is strong and energy is high, the last thing most churches are thinking about is changing a culture.

Leadership teams must involve people through layers of culture-promoting discipleship. The language, stories, and methods we use should ingrain leadership development in their very core. Whatever we celebrate, we will replicate. As church leaders, we are not reactive, but we must be on the offense, not defense, in our proactive approach to discipleship. A defensive approach to discipleship implies that the hearts of the people in your congregation are pure and in need of protection.

In order to see a transformation in our churches, we must aggressively go after the hearts of our churches. To practice discipleship well, we must teach it clearly. And to teach it clearly, we must understand it well. Begin to define what a disciple looks like and then develop a strategy for equipping people.

Invest in a Few People

As you've probably noticed by now—and as Jesus modeled to His disciples and us—this is the way of multiplication (Jesus's Way + Local Church + Biblical Blueprint = Multiplication).

Now what? Where do I begin? The answer is to invest in three people. You should go home, get around a table with three people, and ask them to go with you on a personal journey of discipleship for one full year. Then, if you think your desire is real and that you truly have something to offer the church, invite others to join you on the journey.

We are not talking crazy statistics that you find at a conference; we are talking about investing in just three people. In three years or so, you will have 15 or more people invested. The math works. As Robert Coleman said, "A few people so dedicated in time will shake the world for God. Victory is never won by the multitudes."[4] Although Jesus did what He could to help the multitudes, He devoted Himself primarily to a few men rather than the masses so the masses could, at last, be saved. If you're a discipleship leader, your church will follow. It might take some time, but they will begin to follow you (or they'll get fed up and leave, which is just fine).

You may be saying, "You've got to be kidding me, Jonathan. Why not the entire church?" Most pastors can't handle this and aren't ready for the countercultural model. They will resist, because the model contradicts decades of church ministry models. It may cost them their job.

1. Crowd: The great multitude 150–500 (1/10th of Jesus's time was spent with this group. Therefore, Jesus restricted 9/10th of His time to 12 Jews.)
2. Committed: 70–120 people (Matt. 5, Sermon on the Mount)
3. Community: 12 disciples (Jesus worked the majority of His time with the disciples. Eugene Peterson said, "Jesus spent 90 percent of his life with just a few ordinary people."[5])
4. Cell: Triad group (Peter, John, and James)
5. Called: One-on-one (You will be hard pressed to find Jesus ministering one-on-one in a systematic relationship. He just didn't do it. One-on-one happens outside the group, never in place of the group. Growth explodes as members of the group reproduce.)

Lifeway Research Group found that those in a smaller group context often pray more frequently, give more generously, study the Bible more consistently, and serve more faithfully than those who are in a larger group.[6]

This journey of discipleship with the church will take a tremendous amount of patience, vulnerability, and grace. In our fast-paced, results-driven society, people will push back because it seems as though we are not doing much. It's not flashy and impressive since you can't say that 800 people signed up for a new program. So don't start any programs, don't make announcements, and don't do anything public. Just start small. Disciple a few. That is how Jesus did it. He was not concerned with programs to reach the multitudes but with people whom the multitudes would follow.

Let's Get Busy

A good strategy executed today is better than a perfect plan that might get executed next week. We must choose to say, "I'm not sacrificing the discipleship of leaders, which is my primary job. It's not about getting the job done, but truly investing." G. K. Chesterton, a Christian philosopher, said it well: "Anything worth doing is worth doing badly."[7]

As leaders, let's challenge other believers not only with our exhortations but also with our example. And let's take great confidence in the gospel, "for it is the power of God for salvation" (Rom. 1:16). It is a biblical mandate for all to witness and make disciples. "Everyone to whom much was given, of him much will be required" (Luke 12:48). We have been given no greater gift than the gospel, and we have no greater stewardship than to share that message of good news with others. All our lives belong to our heavenly father.

> A good strategy executed today is better than a perfect plan that might get executed next week.

Our churches are brimming with too many people who are full of themselves and not Christ. Until we admit that we don't know everything, we can't learn anything. A disciple must be teachable. We have enough people who are benchwarmers. Let's get out of our seats and go into the streets. It's time for a fresh wind in our cities. We must win souls for Christ and have victory for Jesus, but there will be no victory without a battle.

We need to step it up. We need to toughen up and take this job seriously. We need to be ready to suffer for the gospel. We need

> Refusing to embrace a biblical mandate of making disciples is a heart issue, not a head issue—a lack of passion, not a lack of knowledge.

to be motivated by this stewardship with which we have been entrusted. We are to run this race well. So what is holding you back? Refusing to embrace a biblical mandate of making disciples is a heart issue, not a head issue—a lack of passion, not a lack of knowledge. Let's get busy. Let's do this. Let's go live out what we are called to do—to equip saints for the work of the ministry.

Notes

Foreword

1. Daniel Im, *No Silver Bullets: Five Small Shifts that will Transform Your Ministry* (Nashville: B&H Publishing, 2018), 33.

Introduction

1. Bill Bright, *Have You Heard of the Four Spiritual Laws?* (New Life Resources, 2005), 2.
2. The Barna Group, George Barna, and David Kinnaman, eds., *Churchless: Understanding Today's Unchurched and How to Connect with Them* (Carol Stream, IL: Tyndale Momentum, 2016).
3. John Piper (tweet), https://twitter.com/johnpiper/status/5027319857?lang=en.
4. Proverb quoted in Richard Alan Krieger, *Civilization's Quotations : Life's Ideal* (New York: Algora Publishing, 2002), 280.

Chapter 1

1. David T. Olson, *The American Church in Crisis: Groundbreaking Research Based on a National Database of over 200,000 Churches* (Grand Rapids, MI: Zondervan, 2008).
2. Ed Stetzer and Thom S. Rainer, *Transformational Church: Creating a New Scorecard for Congregations* (Nashville, TN: B&H Publishing Group, 2010).
3. Ed Stetzer and Daniel Im, *Planting Missional Churches: Your Guide to Starting Churches That Multiply* (Nashville, TN: B&H Academic, 2016).

4. Dave Browning, *Deliberate Simplicity: How the Church Does More by Doing Less* (Grand Rapids, MI: Zondervan, 2009), 43.

5. D.A. Carson, *Christ and Culture Revisited* (Grand Rapids, MI: Wm. B. Eerdmans Publishing, 2008).

6. J. D. Payne, *Apostolic Church Planting: Birthing New Churches from New Believers* (Downers Grove, IL: InterVarsity Press, 2015).

7. Dietrich Bonhoeffer, *The Cost of Discipleship* (New York: Touchstone, 1995), 59, quoted in Jonathan Parnell, "Christianity without Discipleship Is Christianity without Christ," January 29, 2012, *Desiring God*, https://www.desiringgod.org/articles/christianity-without-discipleship-is-christianity-without-christ.

8. "LifeWay Adults," *Disciples Path* (LifeWay Press, 2015).

9. Jim Putman, *Real-Life Discipleship: Building Churches That Make Disciples* (Colorado Springs, CO: NavPress, 2010).

10. Daniel Im, *No Silver Bullets: 5 Small Shifts That Will Transform Your Ministry* (Nashville, TN: B&H Publishing Group, 2017).

11. Bill Hull, *Conversion & Discipleship: You Can't Have One without the Other* (Grand Rapids, MI: Zondervan, 2006), 19.

12. John MacArthur, *Twelve Ordinary Men: How the Master Shaped His Disciples for Greatness, and What He Wants to Do with You* (Nashville, TN: Thomas Nelson, 2006).

13. C.S. Lewis, *Mere Christianity*, (New York: Harper Collins, 1989), 199.

14. Barna Group, *Barna Trends 2017: What's New and What's Next at the Intersection of Faith and Culture* (Grand Rapids, MI: Baker Books, 2016).

15. Robby Gallaty, *Rediscovering Discipleship: Making Jesus' Final Words Our First Work* (Grand Rapids, MI: Zondervan, 2015).

16. Gallaty, *Rediscovering Discipleship*, 40.

17. Dietrich Bonhoeffer, *The Cost of Discipleship*, 43.

Chapter 2

1. Diana West, *The Death of the Grown-Up: How America's Arrested Development Is Bringing Down Western Civilization* (New York: St. Martin's Griffin, 2008), 14.
2. Iain H. Murray, *The Forgotten Spurgeon* (Edinburgh: Banner of Truth, 2009).
3. Scot McKnight, *The King Jesus Gospel: The Original Good News Revisited* (Grand Rapids, MI: Zondervan, 2016), 14.
4. Bill Hull, *Conversion & Discipleship: You Can't Have One without the Other* (Grand Rapids, MI: Zondervan, 2016).
5. J. D. Greear, *Stop Asking Jesus into Your Heart: How to Know for Sure You Are Saved* (Nashville, TN: B&H Publishing Group, 2013).
6. Matthew W. Bates, *Salvation by Allegiance Alone: Rethinking Faith, Works, and the Gospel of Jesus the King* (Grand Rapids, MI: Baker Academic, 2017).
7. Eric Metaxas, *Martin Luther: The Man Who Rediscovered God and Changed the World* (New York: Penguin Random House, 2017).
8. Bonhoeffer, *The Cost of Discipleship.*
9. A.W. Tozer, *The Pursuit of God* (CreateSpace Independent Publishing Platform, 2016).
10. Dietrich Bonhoeffer, *Life Together: The Classic Exploration of Christian in Community* (New York: Harper & Row Publishers, 1954), 454.
11. R.C. Sproul and Stephen J. Nichols, *The Legacy of Luther* (Sanford, FL: Reformation Trust Publishing, 2016).
12. Ligonier Ministries, *Luther and the Reformation* (Orlando, FL; Ligonier Ministries, 2017).
13. John Calvin, *Institutes of the Christian Religion* (Peabody, MA: Hendrickson Publishers, 2007).
14. Wayne Grudem, *Systematic Theology: An Introduction to Biblical Doctrine* (Leicester, Great Britain: Zondervan, 1994).
15. Thomas Schreiner, *Faith Alone: The Doctrine of Justification: What Reformers Taught . . . and Why It Still Matters* (Grand Rapids, MI: Zondervan, 2015).

16. Andrew M. Davis, *An Infinite Journey: Growing toward Christlikeness* (Greenville, SC: Emerald House, 2014).

17. Bob Kellemen and Kevin Carson, eds., *Biblical Counseling and the Church: God's Care through God's People* (Grand Rapids, MI: Zondervan, 2015).

18. C.S. Lewis, *The Screwtape Letters* (New York: Harper Collins, 2015), 5.

19. JR Woodward and Dan White Jr., *The Church As Movement: Starting and Sustaining Missional-Incarnational Communities* (Downers Grove, IL: InterVarsity Press, 2016), 28.

20. David Platt, *Follow Me: A Call to Die. A Call to Live* (Carol Stream, IL: Tyndale House Publishers, 2013).

21. Jonathan K. Dodson, *Gospel-Centered Discipleship* (Wheaton, IL: Crossway, 2012).

22. Bill Hull and Ben Sobels, *The Discipleship Gospel: What Jesus Preached — We Must Follow* (HIM Publications, 2018).

23. Dallas Willard, *The Divine Conspiracy: Rediscovering Our Hidden Life in God* (San Francisco: HarperSanFrancisco, 1998).

24. Jerry Bridges, *The Discipline of Grace: God's Role and Our Role in the Pursuit of Holiness* (Colorado Springs, CO: NavPress, 2006), 59.

25. Charles Spurgeon, "A Sermon Intended for Reading on Lord's Day, October 26, 1902" (sermon presented at New Park Street Chapel, Southwark, during the winter of 1860–1861), https://www.ccel.org/ccel/spurgeon/sermons48.xliii.html.

Chapter 3

1. Eugene H. Peterson, *A Long Obedience in the Same Direction: Discipleship in an Instant Society* (Downers Grove, IL: IVP Books, 2000).

2. Mark Dever, *Discipling: How to Help Others Follow Jesus* (Wheaton, IL: Crossway, 2016).

3. Francis Chan with Danae Yankoski, *Crazy Love: Overwhelmed by a Relentless God* (Colorado Springs, CO: David C. Cook, 2013), 8.

4. Matt Chandler and Jared C. Wilson, *The Explicit Gospel* (Wheaton, IL: Crossway, 2012).

5. Alvin L. Reid, *Sharing Jesus without Freaking Out: Evangelism the Way You Were Born to Do It* (Nashville, TN: B&H Academic, 2017).

6. Robert E. Coleman, *The Master Plan of Evangelism* (Grand Rapids, MI: Revell, 2010).

7. Dever, *Discipling: How to Help Others Follow Jesus.*

Chapter 4

1. C.S. Lewis, *The Four Loves* (San Francisco: HarperOne, 2017), 121.

2. David Platt, *Counter Culture: Following Christ in an Anti-Christian Age* (Carol Stream, IL: Tyndale House Publishers, 2015).

3. Henri J.M. Nouwen, Donald P. McNeill, and Douglas A. Morrison, *Compassion: A Reflection on the Christian Life* (New York: Image, 2006).

4. Rick Rusaw and Brian Mavis, *The Neighboring Church: Getting Better at What Jesus Said Matters Most* (Nashville, TN: Thomas Nelson, 2016).

5. Alex Murashko, "EXCLUSIVE Rick Warren: 'Flat Out Wrong' That Muslims, Christians View God the Same," March 2, 2012, *The Christian Post*, https://www.christianpost.com/news/exclusive-rick-warren -flat-out-wrong-that-muslims-christians-view-god-the-same-70767/.

6. Bobby Jamieson, *Going Public: Why Baptism Is Required for Church Membership* (Nashville, TN: B&H Publishing, 2015).

7. Mark Dever and Jonathan Leeman, eds., *Baptist Foundations: Church Government for an Anti-Institutional Age* (Nashville, TN: B&H Publishing, 2015).

8. Jason Allen, ed., *The SBC and the 21st Century: Reflection, Renewal, & Recommitment* (Nashville, TN: B&H Academic, 2016).

9. Thom S. Rainer, *I Am a Church Member: Discovering the Attitude That Makes the Difference* (Nashville, TN: B&H Publishing, 2013).

10. John M. Frame, *The Doctrine of the Word of God* (Phillipsburg, NJ: P&R Publishing, 2010).

11. Francis Chan with Mark Beuving, *Multiply: Disciples Making Disciples* (Colorado Springs, CO: David C. Cook, 2012).

12. Jonathan Leeman, *Church Membership: How the World Knows Who Represents Jesus* (Wheaton, IL: Crossway, 2012).

13. Dever and Leeman, eds., *Baptist Foundations*.

14. James MacDonald, Bob Kellemen, and Steve Viars, *Christ-Centered Biblical Counseling: Changing Lives with God's Changeless Truth* (Eugene, OR: Harvest House Publishers, 2013).

15. Dever, *Discipling: How to Help Others Find Jesus*, 68.

16. Eric Geiger, "5 Steps to Simplifying Your Church's Schedule," *Eric Geiger*, Oct. 3, 2016, https://ericgeiger.com/2016/10/5-steps-to-simplifying -your-churchs-schedule/.

Chapter 5

1. Dallas Willard, *The Spirit of the Disciplines: Understanding How God Changes Lives* (San Francisco: HarperOne, 1999).

2. Joe Gibbs with Jerry B. Jenkins, *Game Plan for Life: Your Personal Playbook for Success* (Carol Stream, IL: Tyndale House Publishers, 2011).

3. Charles Spurgeon, quoted in Jason Daye, "Christian George: What Charles Spurgeon Has to say to the Church Today," April 12, 2017, *ChurchLeaders*, https://churchleaders.com/podcast/302145-christian -george-charles-spurgeon-say-church-today.html.

4. Thom S. Rainer and Eric Geiger, *Simple Church: Returning to God's Process for Making Disciples* (Nashville, TN: B&H Books, 2011).

5. Robby Gallaty, *Bearing Fruit: What Happens When God's People Grow* (Nashville, TN: B&H Publishing, 2017).

6. Coleman, *The Master Plan of Evangelism*.

7. Stephen Drotter, *The Performance Pipeline: Getting the Right Performance at Every Level of Leadership* (San Francisco: John Wiley & Sons, 2011).

8. Jim Putnam, *Real Life Discipleship* (Carol Stream, IL: Tyndale House Publishers, 2010), 60.

Chapter 6

1. John M. Coles, *Breathe Only Love: A Path to God's Presence* (Bloomington, IN: WestBow Press, 2016), 34.

2. James K.A. Smith, *You Are What You Love: The Spiritual Power of Habit* (Grand Rapids, MI: Brazos Press, 2016).

3. Gallaty, *Bearing Fruit*.

4. Bonhoeffer, *The Cost of Discipleship*.

5. E. Stanley Jones, *The Unshakable Kingdom and the Unchanging Person* (Bellingham, WA: McNett Press, 1995).

6. Kevin DeYoung, *Crazy Busy: A (Mercifully) Short Book about a (Really) Big Problem* (Wheaton, IL: Crossway, 2013), 32.

7. Matthew Henry, *Comprehensive Commentary on the Holy Bible: Matthew through John* (Philadelphia, PA: J.B. Lippincott, 1859), 229.

8. Anne M. Gurath, *Turning Inside Out* (Maitland, FL: Xelon Press, 2007), 133.

9. Bonhoeffer, *The Cost of Discipleship*, 45.

10. Jared C. Wilson, *The Imperfect Disciple: Grace for People Who Can't Get Their Act Together* (Grand Rapids, MI: Baker Books, 2017).

Chapter 7

1. David Platt, *Radical: Taking Back Your Faith from the American Dream* (Colorado Springs, CO: Multnomah Books, 2010).

2. John Piper, *Brothers, We Are Not Professionals: A Plea to Pastors for Radical Ministry* (Nashville, TN: B&H Publishing, 2013), 1.

3. Bill Hull, *The Disciple-Making Pastor: Leading Others on the Journey of Faith* (Grand Rapids, MI: Baker Books, 2007), 18.

4. Eric Geiger, Michael Kelley, and Philip Nation, *Transformational Discipleship: How People Really Grow* (Nashville, TN: B&H Publishing, 2012).

5. Brad Bigney, *Gospel Treason: Betraying the Gospel with Hidden Idols* (Phillipsburg, NJ: P&R Publishing, 2012).

6. Robby Gallaty with Randall Collins, *Growing Up: How to Be a Disciple Who Makes Disciples* (Nashville, TN: B&H Publishing, 2013), Google Books.

7. Ed Stetzer and David Putman, *Breaking the Missional Code: Your Church Can Become a Missionary in Your Community* (Nashville, TN: Broadman & Holman Publishers, 2006).

8. Jeff Iorg, *Building Antioch: Your Role in a Transformational Church* (Nashville, TN: LifeWay Press, 2011).

9. Will Mancini, *Church Unique: How Missional Leaders Cast Vision, Capture Culture, and Create Movement* (San Francisco, CA: Jossey-Bass, 2008).

10. D.L. Moody, *To the Work! To the Work! Exhortations to Christians* (Chicago, IL: Moody Publishers, 1884), 70.

11. Steve Miller, *D.L. Moody on Spiritual Leadership* (Chicago, IL: Moody Publishers, 2004).

12. Barna Group, "The Aging of America's Pastors," March 1, 2017, https://www.barna.com/research/aging-americas-pastors/.

13. Thom S. Rainer and Jess Rainer, *The Millennials: Connecting to America's Largest Generation* (Nashville, TN: B&H Publishing Group, 2011).

14. "Q&A Webinar with Daniel Im on Discipleship from a Systems Perspective," August 31, 2017, *New Churches*, https://newchurches .com/webinars/qa-webinar-daniel-im-discipleship-systems-perspective/.

Chapter 8

1. Rodney Starks, *The Rise of Christianity: How the Obscure, Marginal Jesus Movement Became the Dominant Religious Force in the Western World in a Few Centuries* (Princeton: Princeton University Press, 1996).

2. Daniel Im, "Discipleship Strategy for Multiplication," The Midwest Leadership Summit: Midwest Advance 2018, January 24, 2018, https:// mwadvance.org/conferences/spiritual-awakening-track/.

3. Eric Geiger and Kevin Peck, *Designed to Lead: The Church and Leadership Development* (Nashville, TN: B&H Publishing Group, 2016).

4. Eric Geiger and Kevin Peck, *Designed to Lead*, 39–40, used by permission, all rights reserved.

5. Eric Geiger and Kevin Peck, used by permission, all rights reserved.

6. John C. Maxwell, *The Maxwell Daily Reader: 365 Days of Insight to Develop the Leader within You and Influence Those Around You* (Nashville, TN: Thomas Nelson, 2011), 25.

7. R. Albert Mohler Jr., quoted in Gary Bredfeldt, *Great Leader, Great Teacher: Recovering the Biblical Vision for Leadership* (Chicago, IL: Moody Publishers, 2006), 7.

8. John C. Maxwell, *Be A People Person: Effective Leadership Through Effective Relationships* (Colorado Springs, CO: David C Cook, 2013), 78.

9. Bill Hull, *Conversion and Discipleship: You Can't Have One without the Other* (Grand Rapids, MI: Zondervan, 2006).

10. Peter F. Drucker, *The Effective Executive: The Definitive Guide to Getting the Right Things Done* (New York: HarperCollins Publishers, 2006).

11. Ed Stetzer, *Planting Missional Churches* (Nashville, TN: Broadman & Holman Publishers, 2006).

12. Jim Collins, *Good to Great: Why Some Companies Make the Leap... and Others Don't* (New York: HarperBusiness, 2001).

13. Daniel Meyer, *Witness Essentials: Evangelism That Makes Disciples* (Downers Grove, IL: InterVarsity Press, 2012), 93.

Conclusion

1. Jim Putman, Bill Krause, Avery Willis, and Brandon Guindon, *Real-Life Discipleship Training Manual: Equipping Disciples Who Make Disciples*, (Colorado Springs, CO: NavPress, 2010), 13.

2. "The Westminster Confession of Faith," *Center for Reformed Theology and Apologetics*, http://www.reformed.org/documents/wcf_with_proofs/.

3. Theodore Gerhardt Tappert, ed., *The Book of Concord: The Confessions of the Evangelical Lutheran Church* (Minneapolis, MN: Fortress Press, 1959), 345.

4. Coleman, *The Master Plan of Evangelism, 32.*

5. Bill Donahue, *Building a Church of Small Groups: A Place Where Nobody Stands Alone* (Grand Rapids, MI: Zondervan, 2001), 145.

6. Stetzer and Rainer, *Transformational Church.*

7. Dale Ahlquist, *G.K. Chesterton: The Apostle of Common Sense*, (San Francisco, CA: Ignatius Press, 2003), 23.

CPSIA information can be obtained
at www.ICGtesting.com
Printed in the USA
BVHW091239131118
532891BV00012B/588/P